Improvised Drama

Improvised Drama

Peter Chilver

B T Batsford Ltd

Printed and bound in Great Britain by
Jarrold and Sons Ltd
London and Norwich
for the publishers
B T BATSFORD LTD
4 Fitzhardinge Street London W1

Contents

6

7

Foreword

This book is intended for classes and groups who are engaged in the study of English or Drama and who are interested to do some kind of improvised drama. The book does not attempt to lay down a 'course' in improvisation, but simply to provide a wide repertoire of ideas from which immediately to start improvising. These ideas are drawn from an equally wide range of sources—from situations suggested by young people in drama sessions, from historical incidents, from law court cases, from plays and novels, operas and ballets, from incidents reported in newspapers—and the aim is to show that improvisation is not something which exists in a department all of its own or is limited simply to the study of drama, but is an imaginative way of using the language and one which can and should spill over into the study of history, of current affairs, of all aspects of literature, and of life itself. There is nothing unusual about improvisation—every conversation is an improvisation—and there is nothing new about it. The first person who ever sat down to tell a story was improvising. And the first children who played games of 'let's pretend' were creating the first kind of improvised drama. Language, speech, improvisation and drama are all a part of each other.

Introduction

The value of improvisation

The interest that has been shown in recent years in improvisation, in the professional theatre and in education, can be traced to the work and writings of a Russian actor and producer, Konstantin Stanislavski, who made extensive use of improvisation as a way of training young actors and as a way of producing and rehearsing a play. It might be said that Stanislavski made three important discoveries about improvised drama:

1 It is enjoyable and exciting for the actors themselves.
2 It develops the actor's imagination.
3 It increases the actor's understanding of any play he may be working on.

The obvious implications of this in the teaching of language and literature are at long last being realised.

What is improvisation?

We create an improvisation whenever we communicate with another person and without having previously rehearsed or memorised what we say or do, or without having the words or actions written down in front of us. Every form of communication is initially an improvisation. An improvisation becomes an improvised drama as soon as it is deliberately enacted for the benefit of others—the audience. All you need, basically, is one actor and one person to sit in the audience. Thus, as Freud pointed out, to make a joke is to create a kind of theatre—improvised drama. This does not mean that improvised drama is intrinsically better than written drama, or that if every schoolchild was encouraged to improvise scenes of his own devising then every schoolchild would automatically achieve high scholastic standards in literature, or produce plays the equal of Shaw's or Shakespeare's. What it does mean is that improvisation is a very basic and instinctive way of using the language, and one which actually aids the development of language. It must therefore incidentally aid the development of the three chief functions of language: thought, imagination, and communication.

What kind of improvisation?

Many of the most insistent advocates of improvisation, in education and in the theatre, seem to be of the opinion that the only really 'valid' form of improvising is one where the performers are deeply involved—emotionally and spiritually—in the drama they are creating. According to this school of thought, improvisation must always be reaching for the serious commitment of the performers. And many writers go so far as to say that it is only by this means that the performer, whether he be a schoolchild or a professional actor, can come to terms with his own self and ultimately hope to lead a basically happy and secure life. The evidence that such writers can refer to is rather dubious, especially as it is impossible to say when a performer is 'seriously involved'. Does this mean that an actor who comes off stage convinced that he has just murdered Desdemona is seriously involved, while a young schoolboy who has just created a hilarious improvisation based on the Punch and Judy theme, is not?

The question is worth asking because our attitude towards it will tend to dominate our attitude towards both the material which we suggest as a basis for improvisations, and towards the way in which we see the material being interpreted. If we are encouraging say a group of teenagers to create improvised drama, should we privately hope that they will start pouring their secret fears and fantasies into their improvisations, under the conviction that in this way we can come to understand them as human beings and help them to overcome their inner spiritual anguish? Or should we joyfully sit back and roar with laughter at the wit and whimsy of one hilarious improvisation after another?

And before we try to answer this question, we may well ask another that is intimately tied up with it. Should any of us, whether teacher or group leader or what you will, attempt to 'mark' other people's improvisations? After all, the teaching of English in schools would totally disintegrate if teachers were stopped suddenly from giving marks to pupil's 'essays'—for what else can you do with an essay but give it a mark?—are we, then, to do the same thing with improvised drama? If not, what else is there to do with it? The answer to this question is easier than one might suppose, and is apparent to anyone who has ever participated in any capacity in a session of improvisation: there is no need for a teacher's 'mark' because an improvisation is essentially the property of the entire audience, and the audience's reaction, whether in terms of laughter or silence or exclamatory gasps, is itself the criticism that the performers are looking for. In fact, because it usually takes more than one to improvise, each performer is himself actively involved in the criticism of the piece. An improvisation-session in which only the teacher or the leader is criticising is a contradiction in terms.

But should the audience be laughing or crying? Should the drama they are witnessing be escapist fantasy or Brechtian realism? Should we suggest to children of nine that they improvise scenes in which they murder their little sister? (after all, many children apparently have a great urge to murder their little sister) or should we suggest a scene in which they take their little sister to the cinema and she keeps on getting up to go to the toilet? Or should we keep to the land of Noddy? Or should we suggest nothing?

For the answer we have only to look at the history of improvisation and at a group of people actually improvising. Historically the connection between improvisation and comedy is a remarkable one. As Eric Bentley points out, one hears of the *Commedia dell'Arte* but not of a *Tragedia dell'Arte*. This does not mean that we do not make intensely serious points when we create improvised farce or improvised satire, but simply that we make them in the form of comedy and not of tragedy. That improvisation tends to bring out the satirist in all of us is, I believe, apparent to anyone who has ever 'improvised'. This does not mean that we should avoid any kind of 'serious' improvisation. In fact, quite a large number of the ideas suggested in this book are invitations to be 'serious'. But it does mean that we should never try to dictate the mood in which a group attempt to improvise, or even to persuade by more subtle means.

What standard should be aimed at?

After a fair amount of improvising most groups will show:

1 A readiness of response to given material and a marked ability to provide material for themselves.

2 The ability to sustain an idea and develop it.

3 A critical appreciation of the work of others and of themselves.

What does it lead to?

It can develop a greater command of the language (oral and written) and a wide interest in theatre and in all forms of literature. It also incidentally provides a rich source of ideas for written work. For this reason many teachers follow a session in improvisation with a session in writing.

How to start

Divide the students into groups—letting people work as far as possible with the people they want to work with—give them some material to work on, and then let the groups work simultaneously. Afterwards encourage the groups to show their work to the rest, but do not force this.

What facilities are needed?

The more space the better. The occasional rostra or stage blocks are also useful, and if you have any available, just leave them out for people to use as they choose. But it can be done in very confined spaces. Where there's a will, there's a way.

How to use this book

Do not attempt to use the book methodically. Try a couple of ideas from one part of the book and then switch to another. Not all of the material will be equally successful with all kinds of groups. But the more experienced a group become, the more they will be able to cope with different kinds of basic material.

Talk about it

Creating improvised drama is not like going to the theatre. You are not supposed to sit still and silent and then clap politely at the end. The improvisation can be stopped at any point to talk about it. If the actors exhaust their imagination they can legitimately turn round and ask for assistance. Nor do improvisations have to have traditional 'endings'—they may simply stop or fade out. Talk and talk further about an improvisation. Then perhaps do it again. It is also an excellent idea, once the group have become really experienced, to make it a rule that others may walk into the improvisation even when they are not members of that particular group.

I

Improvisations based on situations

I Improvisations based on situations

Introductory note

The group are given the details of each situation and are then asked to improvise its dramatic development. Any aspect of the situation can be taken as the basis of the improvisation and the situation does not have to be interpreted literally or faithfully. For instance, the age and sex of the characters can be changed, or the time and place. The situation merely provides a basic theme on which to work.

The situations are given in four sections:
- (i) General Situations, including situations based on incidents recently reported in newspapers.
- (ii) Situations based on Historical Events.
- (iii) Situations based on Court Cases.
- (iv) Situations based on incidents in Plays, Operas and Ballets.

(i) General situations

Incident on a Bus

In September 1966 the newspapers reported the following incident: A small child was travelling on a bus to visit a friend. She had a box with her in which she had a pet white mouse, four weeks old. The bus conductor collected an eightpenny fare from the child in the normal way, and then asked for an extra fare of sevenpence for the white mouse. The conductor explained that the white mouse was 'livestock' and that livestock must be paid for. The extra money was paid by the child's grandfather who was travelling with her. Some time later, after various complaints had been made about the incident, a bus company official visited the child's home, refunded the sevenpenny fare, and made an official apology.

Improvise the scene on the bus. Admit plenty of fellow passengers. Improvise the later scene, where the official returns the extra fare.

Hypnosis and Outer Space

In October 1966 newspapers in America reported that a husband and wife had recently been driving through the countryside when they saw a light moving in the sky. At first they thought it was a plane, but the light came nearer and nearer to the earth, and then the couple realised that it was some kind of flying saucer. The object landed in a nearby field and the couple got out of their car and went over to have a look at it. From that moment the couple can remember absolutely nothing until two days later they woke up in the field to find that the object had disappeared. The couple went to see a hypnotist who put them in a trance, and when under the trance they were able to piece together the details of what had happened in the two missing days. . . . What had happened?

Improvise the scene at the hypnotist's, with both the husband and wife preparing for the hypnosis.

Election Time

You are a political candidate at a General Election and are going from door to door canvassing for votes. At each door a different situation presents itself.

Improvise the candidate's experiences.

Teachers and Pupils

At many schools all the pupils and one or both of their parents are interviewed by the Headmaster or senior master before the pupil is formally admitted to the school.

Improvise a scene in which a mother arrives for such an interview accompanied by her son Tommy. Mother tries to warn the Headmaster that Tommy is a great nuisance and that she can do nothing with him and doubts very much if the school will be able to either.

Improvise the same situation except that the mother on this occasion wants to make it quite clear that her Tommy is a model pupil, and is perfect in every way, and that no one must ever suggest anything to the contrary. Improvise further variations on the same basic idea.

Conversation in a Restaurant

You are sitting alone in a quiet restaurant, eating a meal, when a stranger comes in and sits beside you. He orders a meal and starts a conversation about the weather. When his meal arrives he continues talking with you, and then leans across for the salt and pepper. A few seconds later he leans across again, and in the most polite manner possible removes a potato from your plate and starts eating it.

Improvise the story up to this point, and then develop it.

Lions for the Stately Home

An English Peer has recently purchased a number of lions which he intends to keep on his estate with a view to their being a 'side-show' to attract visitors to his Stately Home. His venture has attracted quite a lot of criticism, especially from people who live near the estate and consider that the lions are too dangerous. The Peer has insisted that the lions will never be able to escape from his custody and that the local people therefore have nothing to fear.

Improvise a meeting between the Peer and a group of local citizens who have come to make a protest.

Improvise the same meeting at some future date, imagining that at that time the lions have in fact escaped.

Late Nights

Joe, a sixteen-year-old, has gone out to a friend's birthday party. His father, who considers his son a frivolous character living only for a 'good time', has permitted him to go on the strict understanding that he will be back home by eleven at the latest. His mother has made Joe promise that he will be home at the time the father has requested, and has bribed him with a £1 note in return for the promise. The father as yet knows nothing of the £1 bribe. The time is just after midnight. Mother has gone to bed, and so has younger brother Ted. Suddenly Father shouts up noisily from downstairs that Joe has still not come home.

Improvise the story from this point.

Castaways

In the summer of 1966 a group of six Tongan youths were rescued from an uninhabited Pacific island where they had been shipwrecked for fifteen months. The castaways had laid down strict rules for themselves in order to keep themselves alive, and had shown tremendous resource and imagination. They had built a hut in the crater of an extinct volcano, had made a guitar from coconuts and from the wire of their own wrecked whaleboat, had written songs about their adventures and had eaten the raw flesh of sea birds and drunk their blood to compensate for the lack of drinking water. They had regular sessions of prayer and maintained a non-stop system of watch-keeping. They saw four different ships sail past the island before they were able to attract the attention of one and so get back to civilisation.

Improvise some of their adventures. Change the characters of the castaways and see what might have happened if one of the group had been uncooperative and had tried to dominate. Then improvise the situation with characters from very different backgrounds. (Now read *The Lord of the Flies* by William Golding.)

A Case for the Magistrate

A pupil at a London secondary school was recently charged by the police with cycling across a safety crossing while it was being used by a pedestrian. It appeared that the road was a particularly wide one and that on the occasion in question only one pedestrian was using the crossing—an elderly lady who was at the opposite side of the crossing to the cyclist. There was no possibility of an accident occurring. Nevertheless a policeman saw the incident, called out to the cyclist—who stopped—and charged him. The pupil was a young man of sixteen, with an excellent school record. His Headmaster offered to appear in court to testify to his good character and when he did so he informed the Magistrate that the young man was one of the five or six best pupils who had ever passed through the school. He added that the following year the pupil would undoubtedly be made Head Prefect of the school, that he had obtained ten GCE 'O' Levels the previous summer, and that he would be going on to University within the next couple of years. The pupil's father testified that his son was a very quiet and law-abiding person and was if anything too much inclined to keep to the 'straight and narrow' and was in this respect unlike his younger brother who was much more rebellious and uncontrollable. At the same time the father commented that the police are quite willing to close their eyes to millions of motorists who drive over safety crossings when pedestrians are half-way across, and he could not understand why his son should have been singled out on this occasion.

The Magistrate gave the pupil a conditional discharge.

Improvise the scene in the Magistrate's Court.

The Canterbury Tales

In Chaucer's *Canterbury Tales* a group of travellers entertain each other on a long journey by telling each other stories. Improvise a similar situation.

Improvise a situation in which the story-tellers, instead of telling stories about different characters, tell the stories of their own lives.

His First Day at Work

A young man goes off to his first day's work after leaving school—as an assistant salesman at a supermarket. He recognises a girl he knows working at a counter quite near to his own. Improvise some of his day's experiences. Improvise the scene in the early morning when he has to get up rather earlier than he used to in his school-days. Improvise the scene a few weeks previously when he had just left school and had no particular idea what he would do with himself and was eventually made to discuss the matter with his mother and father. Improvise the scene in the evening of his first day, when he returns home from work and his parents want to know how he got on.

Improvise the same basic situation but this time vary the kind of job and the character of the young man.

The Old School Tie

When Charles and Harry were at school they were believed to be the best of friends, but were in fact bitter rivals and very nearly enemies.

When Harry was made a prefect and Charles was not, Charles left school in a fit of pique and irritation and the two never met again. Now twenty years later and with many changes of fortune in the years between, Harry arrives for an interview with the owner of a large manufacturing company to whom he has applied for a job as a departmental manager. The job has been advertised in the national press, and Harry has no idea that the owner is his old rival, Charles.

Improvise the interview.

Improvise the same situation with the rôles changed round, i.e. with Charles as the applicant.

Improvise around similar circumstances but with varied situations. For example, let the two meet in the Army, or on a secret military operation, or at a party given by their wives who are also old school friends.

The Girl-friend Problem

David is sixteen and is due to leave school at the end of next term, after taking his CSE, and a couple of GCEs. He has recently met a girl who works as a shorthand typist in a local office and the two have become firm friends. They meet every Saturday evening and go dancing at the local 'Palais' and go to the cinema every Sunday. David's parents do not approve of the girl (Susan) though they cannot quite make up their minds what it is they disapprove of.

Improvise a scene where David is getting ready early one Saturday evening to go off and meet Susan, and his parents attempt to impress their views on David and try to dissuade him from seeing any more of her.

Then improvise the scene with changes in the personalities of the father, mother and son. Then introduce the character of Susan who has come round to call for David on her way to the Palais.

Improvise a scene a little later in the evening. David and Susan are out at the Palais, and David's parents are watching television when there is a knock on the door. It is Susan's father. . . .

Improvise a scene with David and Susan at the Palais.

The Open Road

Tom and Bill are sixteen and are bored with going on holiday with their respective families to some noisy and dreary seaside resort. They have informed their friends that this year they are going to do something more adventurous and invigorating. They are going to hitch-hike to whatever place they can reach, as far away as possible. They do not mind where, and they do not mind what inconveniences they have to put up with on the way. They intend to spend their nights sleeping in Youth Hostels, or, if needs be, in fields.

Improvise a scene where Tom and Bill have been hiking around for several days, and are now spending the night in a rather depressing boarding house. Tom has found the holiday very exciting but wants to return home for a week or two 'for various reasons' and then perhaps continue the holiday later. He has also found 'the open road' more expensive than he had expected and is down to his last pound, which will just about cover the cost of bed and breakfast. Bill also has found the holiday exciting and wants to continue it, but is feeling a shade depressed tonight on account of a sudden bout of toothache. Until this moment there has been no question of their turning back. But Tom begins to grumble about the boarding house and the landlady. . . .

Improvise the scene the following morning when Tom phones up his mother—reversed charges—and asks her to arrange, somehow, for him to return home in comfort, by train. He explains that she has only to phone the police in the town where he is staying and then he could be on the train within a matter of hours.

Improvise a scene some weeks later when Tom and Bill reminisce on their holiday to their friends.

Knowledge for Sale

You have taken a job as a door-to-door salesman with a firm who sell encyclopaedias. You have been taught the 'spiel', i.e. a very lengthy script which you are supposed to follow from the moment the unsuspecting householder opens the door, *and which begins*: 'Good evening, Madam (or Sir, as the case may be), I wonder if you remember me. Last year I called on you on behalf of my employers who are in charge of market research in this area. No, I don't suppose you do remember me, but here I am again. And this year we are conducting an inquiry into the sort of books the public like to read. I should like to make it clear, Madam, that this is strictly a non-profit-making venture on the part of my employers and there is no question of my trying to sell you anything. . . .' And the 'spiel' progresses from this innocent-sounding overture to a high-powered sales-talk, by slow but careful stages. Your instructions are, whenever a client argues, disagrees, or fails to co-operate, that you should keep on going over the point which you happen to have reached until the client gives way. Then, and only then, do you progress to the next stage.

Improvise various scenes around this basic situation.

Victim

Two young men stand talking on a railway underground station. It is late evening. They are apparently enjoying some kind of joke and are laughing very exuberantly and in so doing are making a good deal of noise. A rather older man who has a quiet and rather fussy appearance goes up to the two young men and asks them not to make so much noise. He tells them they are disturbing other people on the platform. The young men immediately stop talking and appear to say nothing further to each other. But when the train arrives they enter the same compartment as the man who has told them off, and sit opposite him. While the older man opens his newspaper and starts to read, the other two stare straight at him, coolly and without saying anything. The train stops at various stations but the two young men show no sign of leaving. They continue to stare at the other man, who by this time is beginning to be thoroughly scared. Then the older man comes to his station. He gets up to leave the compartment. Without saying anything the two young men proceed to follow him. . . .

Improvise the incident and its sequel.

Dick Turpin, Highwayman

One of the the many legends that have grown up around the name of Dick Turpin, the celebrated highwayman of the eighteenth century, is as follows. One day, when the reward offered for his capture was higher than it had ever been before, Turpin and his gang were refreshing themselves at a wayside inn when a very elegant gentleman came and sat beside them and engaged them in pleasant conversation about the weather and the state of the country. Then he suddenly told them, in no more than a whisper, that he knew who they were and that he had come to them with a special message from King George. The message was to the effect that the King was experiencing a terrible but secret crisis and that he believed Dick Turpin could help him. Would Turpin and his gang accompany the gentleman back to the King's Palace where, at a private and secret meeting, the King would explain his difficulties. . . .

Improvise what happens next.

A Kind of Charity

A young man takes up his first job since leaving school—as a trainee news reporter on a weekly newspaper in a small town. One of his first assignments is to report the morning's cases at the local magistrate's court. Among these cases is one involving a young man charged with and convicted of stealing a motor car and driving it away while under the influence of alcohol. It appears that the offender was of previous good character, and that the event would never have occurred had he not become drunk at a party and been 'dared' to do something adventurous. While the young reporter is writing up the morning's cases back at the newspaper office, the father of the convicted man comes to plead with the reporter not to mention the case in the newspaper. He explains that a newspaper report would ruin his son's career and would completely wreck the happiness of his family.

Improvise the scene between the father and the young reporter. See how many different kinds of argument and persuasion could be employed in such an instance. Vary the characters of both the participants.

Surely Not

You are in the middle of a long journey and have just changed trains at a very quiet country station, where there are only two platforms and these face each other with the railway line running in between. You are sitting on a bench waiting for your next train to arrive. Two people are sitting alongside you—a very quiet-looking old man, and an elderly lady who is fast asleep. There are no signs of any porters or station-masters but on the platform opposite is a small group of equally placid people also seated on a bench and presumably waiting for a train. Suddenly you hear a piercing yell, and you see a man emerge from the tunnel that connects the two platforms—he is ordinarily dressed but is carrying a long spear and is apparently impersonating a wild Indian. He charges up the opposite platform, uttering wild cries, and then charges down again. But to your astonishment nobody else appears to notice him. Then he disappears down the tunnel. A second later he reappears—on your own platform.

Improvise the scene.

A Question of Conscience

A fifteen-year-old Australian schoolboy recently refused to continue serving in his school cadet corps as a gesture of protest at his country's involvement in the war in Vietnam.

Improvise a situation in which the pros and cons of the boy's decision can be put forward.

The Interview

A group of people are waiting to be interviewed for a job.

Improvise the situation and the different techniques of conversation which they employ to discourage each other.

(ii) Historical events

N.B. It is essential to have at hand a good series of illustrated social history. Plenty of research should be done before embarking on these improvisations.

The Chimney Sweeps

Almost every major social reform in our history has been achieved only after the most bitter struggle and opposition. A very good example of this was the campaign to stop children and young people from being used for climbing up and cleaning chimneys. Numerous commissions of inquiry were set up by Parliament in the first half of the nineteenth century to report on the conditions of the 'chimney boys' and these revealed the appalling inhumanity of their lives: extreme cruelty had often to be employed in order to get boys to go up chimneys; the dangers of climbing were so great that many thousands were killed by suffocation or by being burned alive; and of those who survived the majority spent the rest of their lives either permanently crippled or seriously diseased. Very few chimney boys lived to be twenty. Even so, the House of Lords defeated numerous Bills which attempted to abolish this practice, and it was not until 1875 that such a Bill passed successfully through both Houses— roughly 100 years after the first attempts at reform. Among the many arguments used in Parliament (and especially in the House of Lords) to defeat the proposed reform were the following:

(i) There was no alternative way of cleaning chimneys.

(ii) If chimneys were not cleaned, then all of England's houses, and especially her stately homes, would catch fire and burn down.

(iii) Employers had a right to employ labour on such terms as they chose, and this included the labour of chimney boys, many of whom were five and six years old.

(iv) Most of the chimney boys were 'unwanted lads' who were apprenticed by the parish to their employers. If the system were abolished the parish would have to continue to support the boys. 'It is better that boys should sweep chimneys than lie idle in the workhouse.'

(v) Such a reform would be an attempt by Parliament to dictate the morals of the country.

(vi) The chimney boys themselves enjoyed their work and grew strong and healthy at it.

(vii) Householders, and especially housewives, did not believe in the efficacy of the brush as a substitute for the chimney boy.

Improvise a House of Lords debate of the time, in which these arguments, and their counter-arguments, are put forward.

Writers of fiction, and some historians also, have tried to reduce the conflicts of the Civil War, and the struggle between the Puritans and the Royalists, to a simple matter of right and wrong. In fact, many different issues were woven into the story, among them: a *religious* issue—established Church versus the Non-Conformists; a *political* one—could the King govern without a duty to consult the people he governed? an *economic* one—by what means, and on what conditions could taxes be levied for the running of the country? and a *personal* one—the personality of Charles I, who believed God to be firmly and unquestionably on his side, and the personality of Oliver Cromwell, equally convinced that God was on his own side. Whatever one may feel about the conflict, no one can deny that Cromwell and his government altered the course of European history and astounded the whole civilised world when in 1649 Charles I was brought to trial by his own subjects, charged with murder, treason and tyranny, found guilty, and executed.

The Court which tried the King was set up by the Puritan members of the House of Commons 'in the name of the Commons in Parliament assembled and all the good people of England'. *The Prosecution Case* was very straightforward—the King was accused of having abused his 'limited power to govern' and of having tried to behave like a tyrant. He had committed murder by waging a war against his own people, and had committed treason by trying to persuade foreign powers to invade the country in order to support his cause.

The *Case for the Defence* was never heard, for the King refused to answer the charge and refused to accept the legality of the Court. Since the King refused to plead either guilty or not guilty, the Court found him guilty and sentenced him to death. The King died nobly, and in so doing won the admiration even of men who were bitterly opposed to his cause. But in the speech he made before his execution, Charles very clearly summed up both his own attitude to the main issue and the issue itself:

'For the people truly I desire their liberty and freedom so much as anybody whatsoever: but I must tell you their liberty and freedom consist in having government . . . not in their having a share in the government: that is nothing appertaining to them. A subject and a sovereign are clearly different things.'

In other words, there had to be a revolution, and the execution of the King, before the country could set forth on the long journey to government by the people. Although Charles never argued his case before the Court we can fairly confidently surmise how he would have answered the various charges which the Puritans brought against him.

Do some research into the events leading up to the Civil War and into the subsequent history of the Cromwellian revolution. If possible read C. V. Wedgwood's account of *The Trial of Charles I*. Then . . .

Improvise an imaginary meeting of Cromwell and Charles at the time of the trial.

Improvise a scene in a country inn where a traveller brings the news of the trial and its outcome. (Have a look at Trevelyan's illustrated *Social History of England* to give colour and detail to your ideas of the period.)

The Six Burghers of Calais

Edward III laid siege to Calais for a whole year before the city surrendered to him. Out of anger with the citizens for resisting for so long, Edward demanded the lives of six of the town's wealthiest burghers (citizens). Six burghers were brought to the King, the ropes already round their necks, and they would have been hanged on the spot if Edward's wife, Philippa, had not pleaded with Edward to spare their lives.

Improvise the scene.
Then read Bernard Shaw's one-act play *The Six of Calais*.

A Capital Charge

During the First World War a number of cases were reported of men who, normally brave and capable soldiers, suddenly and without warning walked away from the line of action, apparently unable to stand any more fighting. Many such men were charged with and convicted of desertion by improvised military courts consisting of the men's own officers, and were executed by a firing squad which consisted of their own friends and fellow-soldiers. The deserters would be given an officer whose job it was to defend the accused, and another officer would be appointed to prosecute. It was rare for a man to be acquitted in such cases for the official line of reasoning was that a man who walked away from the line of action was a coward, and no amount of psychological explanation was able to change this idea.

Improvise a court martial around this situation. The accused would be tried before a panel of officers and the decision would be reached by majority vote.

Now read the play *Hamp* by John Wilson.

Anne of Cleves

Anne of Cleves was Henry VIII's fourth wife, and he married her for political reasons only. At the time there was a possibility of a Catholic alliance on the European continent against Protestant England, and the marriage with Anne, princess of a Protestant German State, was expected to help combat likely hostilities. Henry was shown a portrait of Anne and although she appeared to be no raging beauty she was decidedly pretty, and Henry therefore agreed to marry her. When he went down to Rochester to meet her off the boat he was appalled to find her portrait had grossly flattered her, and that she was plain, plump and uninteresting. He nevertheless married her in January 1540, but had the marriage annulled seven months later when he discovered that the expected Catholic alliance was not after all going to materialise and that the marriage was therefore no longer a political necessity.

Although not pretty, Anne had a good temper and, obviously, a cool head. She lived on in England for many years, on a handsome pension from the government, and led a quiet but seemingly happy life. Henry of course continued his quest for the right wife.

Anne arrived in England speaking no language but her own—Low German. According to legend, Anne and Henry spent such time as they did spend together, either telling each other what they thought of each other in two different languages, or playing cards.

Improvise their first dinner together, the night of Anne's arrival in England.

Flora Macdonald

Flora Macdonald is perhaps the most popular of all the characters associated with the name of the Jacobite Pretender, Bonnie Prince

Charles. In fact, they met only once, when Flora helped the Prince to escape from the Hebrides to the Isle of Skye, by disguising him as an Irish spinning maid, 'Betty Burke'. They separated in Skye, and from there the Prince was eventually able to escape to safety. Flora, however, was afterwards imprisoned in the Tower of London. She was later released, got married, and settled in North Carolina. In her old age she returned to Scotland and died there in 1790. As for the Bonnie Prince he also grew old, but never quite lost hopes of gaining the English throne from the Hanoverians. He lived on the Continent but came back several times to England to hatch plots, none of which came to anything. He died in Rome in 1788, by which time he had become alcoholic, irritable, and generally rather difficult to live with.

Do some research into the life of the Bonnie Prince, and then improvise a newspaper interview for the year 1777, first with Flora Macdonald in Scotland, and then with the Prince in Rome.

Richard III and the Princes in the Tower

Edward IV died in 1483, leaving his young heir, Edward V, aged twelve, in the care of his brother Richard, Duke of Gloucester. According to the legend, Richard, who was physically deformed and evil by nature, instead of caring for his young nephew had him imprisoned in the Tower with his brother Richard, Duke of York. Richard then seized the throne for himself. Shortly after their imprisonment in the Tower both the young Princes disappeared and were never seen again. It was widely believed at the time, and ever since, that Richard had them murdered. Richard's enjoyment of kingship was not, however, to last very long, for after only two years on the throne, during which time numerous powerful groups were actively opposed to him, he was defeated and killed at Bosworth, to be succeeded on the throne by Henry Tudor (Henry VII). In order to leave no doubt in the minds of contemporaries and of posterity that Richard was indeed a villain, Henry decided to resolve the mystery of the two Princes. Their murderers were found—Dighton and Tyrell—and they confessed that Richard had ordered them to murder the Princes, and that they did so by suffocating them as they slept. They buried their bodies at the foot of a staircase in the Tower but Richard had them re-buried by a priest and in a secret place.

In 1498 someone claiming to be one of the Princes—Richard of

York—and known as Perkin Warbeck, led an uprising against Henry VII, was arrested, and executed.

Nearly two hundred years later the skeleton remains of two boys were found under a staircase in the Tower. They were believed to be those of the two Princes and they were removed to Westminster Abbey. But doubts persisted over the centuries as to whether these remains really did have any connection with the vanished Princes, and in 1933 the tomb in the Abbey was re-opened, by special permission, and was found to contain a heap of animal bones plus bones which could conceivably have been children's of the Princes' age.

The mystery can never now be solved. One thing, however, is fairly certain. Richard III was not the villain that he was painted to be by his successor Henry VII, and which he is represented to be in Shakespeare's play *Richard III*. It seems fairly certain that he was not even so deformed as he has been made out to be. Also, he enacted quite a number of liberal and enlightened measures as King, and it is possible that it was in this way that he incurred the opposition of many of the barons.

Do some research into the events of Richard III's reign, and then improvise as many possible variations as you can think of, on the theme of what may have happened on the night when the Princes 'disappeared'.

Mary, Queen of Scots

During her brief reign as Queen of Scotland, Mary Stuart was involved in several remarkable scandals, including the murder of one of her lovers, the murder of her husband, and her subsequent marriage to the man believed to have murdered her husband. She was further disliked for the fact that she was Roman Catholic, while most of her subjects were Presbyterian. She was finally forced to renounce the throne and to flee to England and to beg protection from Queen Elizabeth. In England Mary was 'protected' and in fact imprisoned for eighteen years and was then executed.

The reasons for Mary's execution may be stated simply:

In the event of Elizabeth dying before Mary, then Mary would succeed to the throne of England. Since Mary was Roman Catholic, and Elizabeth and most of her subjects were Protestant, the prospect of a Catholic succeeding to the throne was not a pleasant one.

In those days, religion and politics tended to go together, and it was well known that the various Catholic powers on the European continent were keen to depose Elizabeth and replace her by a Catholic ruler. In such an event, Mary would have been the logical choice for a successor.

There were indeed many plots to overthrow Elizabeth and place Mary on the throne, and Mary was actively involved in these.

Although, looking back now at England in Elizabethan times, the country and the crown may seem to have been very secure, to an Elizabethan this would not have been the case at all. The country was surrounded by powerful and hostile forces, including France, Spain, and the Papacy itself. And shortly after Mary's execution, the country had at last to cope with the long-threatened Spanish invasion. The continued existence of Mary seemed a constant invitation to foreign powers to support her cause and to replace the Protestant and nationalistic Elizabeth with the Catholic and cosmopolitan Mary.

For all these reasons, Elizabeth was many times urged by her advisers and by Parliament, to have Mary executed. But Elizabeth refused to do so for many years, until yet another conspiracy, in which Mary was once again clearly implicated, caused Elizabeth, most reluctantly and hesitantly, to agree to her execution. Mary died with magnificent courage, just as did her grandson, Charles I, in not dissimilar circumstances, sixty years later.

Do some research into the lives of Elizabeth and of Mary. Then improvise a possible meeting between the two Queens, perhaps at the time when the last and fatal conspiracy was discovered. In fact, Mary and Elizabeth never actually met. Then read, if possible, the play *Maria Stuart* by the German dramatist Schiller, in which a meeting between the two is devised and written with great dramatic imagination. In Schiller's play Mary has the advantage of being rather more handsome than Elizabeth, and of enjoying a greater self-confidence because of this. Whether Mary in fact had more assurance than Elizabeth is doubtful. It is, however, certain that both were brilliant women in their own rights. Both were highly educated, Mary in France, and Elizabeth in England. Both, by the standards of any age, were accomplished. Elizabeth spoke many languages with great fluency, including Latin, and had a very wide appreciation of the Arts. On a personal level, perhaps, Mary's life was more dramatic than Elizabeth's, for Elizabeth remained a spinster, while Mary was married three times: her first husband, the French Dauphin, having died while she was still in her teens, her second having been murdered, and her third, having been hounded out of Scotland, died in an asylum on the Continent. But while Mary's life had personal drama, Elizabeth's life had intense drama on a wider scale, as the head of state in an age of great adventure, expansion and change.

Apparently Elizabeth never fully intended Mary to be executed, not even when she signed the execution warrant. She had intended to keep the warrant but to use it as a means of finally discouraging Mary from any further conspiracies. But Elizabeth's advisers took the document without her express permission, and used it to rid the country of a menace.

Wat Tyler

The Peasants' Revolt of 1381 is in many ways one of the first great landmarks in modern European history. Although the revolt ended in failure and the death of its leaders, it marks the first great endeavour to speak out for the rights of man. Very briefly the circumstances of the revolt were these: in the fourteenth century the life of the working man in England both changed and improved; in particular, the Black Death had so reduced the population as to make the individual peasant a more valuable commodity. As a result the old idea of feudalism—in which the peasant was simply the property of the man on whose land he worked—was slowly breaking down. The labourer was now able, for the first time, to move from place to place in order to find better working conditions, and to sell his labour to the highest bidder. The government—King and barons—struck a blow at this development and attempted to turn back the clock with the Statute of Labourers, by which labourers were forbidden to move from place to place, and wages were frozen, and then by the Poll Tax, by which a fairly heavy annual tax was imposed on every single person. This tax was heavy enough to make it impossible for the labourer to keep for himself any profit from his labour. The Peasants' Revolt was an attempt to stop this return to the way things had been and an attempt to retain the relative freedom to which the working man had quite recently become accustomed. The Revolt began in Essex where a tax collector was driven out by a group of labourers. It spread spontaneously to other parts of the country. The Revolt was never a bloodbath in the way most rebellions are—the French Revolution for instance. And when the Queen accidentally drove into a section of the rebel army on the highway she was allowed to pass through unmolested. In fact, the rebellion was not aimed at the King but at the barons who were running the country. The King was Richard II, who was still a boy at the time. And right to the very end the rebels protested their loyalty to him. The purpose of the rebellion was to present the peasants' case to the King and to drive out the barons.

The chief leaders of the rebellion were Wat Tyler and a clergyman, John Ball. It was Ball who gave the classic definition of the aims of the revolt: 'Things cannot go well in England . . . until everything shall be held in common; when there shall neither be vassal nor lord, and all distinctions levelled; when the lords shall be no more masters than ourselves'.

The rebels advanced on London where they met the King at Mile End and asked him to grant the following:

The abolition of serfdom.

The free right to sell labour.

A fixed rent of land at fourpence per acre.

The King readily agreed to this and also agreed that all traitors should be hanged. By traitors the peasants meant, of course, the barons. The King presumably meant the peasants themselves.

At the same time as one group of the rebels met the King at Mile End, another group seized the Tower of London and executed all the nobles they found there. The event was greeted by the Londoners with enthusiasm and largely ignored by most of the barons who were unable for the moment to offer organised resistance because their own armies were so much smaller than those of the peasants. But a second meeting was arranged between King and rebels, this time at Smithfield (also in London). This time Wat Tyler asked for more.

The confiscation of Church land and wealth and the distribution of all this wealth among the ordinary people.

A decree that all men, except the King, were equal.

And once again the King agreed. But at that moment, by arrangement, someone in the King's party called out to Tyler that he was a common thief and highwayman. Tyler demanded to know who it was who was thus accusing and insulting him. When no one answered, Tyler, who was otherwise unarmed, drew out a knife and demanded that his accuser step forward. At the same time he moved forward from his own supporters into the King's party so that he could face his accuser face to face. He was immediately struck down and killed by one of the King's followers on the pretext that he had drawn arms against the King in person. The King called out to the peasants not to panic—'I will be your captain, follow me.' And he arranged for all of them to go away unharmed. The barons were not, however, to be denied their revenge. Their troops swept through London, massacring all who got in their way, and there were many killings up and down the land. Most of the leaders were captured and executed, one of them saying at the scaffold: 'If in the cause of liberty I must die, I shall think myself happy to end my days as a martyr.'

The King never kept the promises he made at Mile End and Smithfield. The rebellion was over. The promises were broken.

Improvise the meeting of the rebels with the King at Mile End and then at Smithfield.

The Scopes Trial

In 1925 the State of Tennessee passed a law which made it unlawful for any educational establishment to teach any account of man's evolution which conflicted with the biblical version. John Scopes, a young biology teacher in a Tennessee high school, broke the law by teaching Darwin's theory of evolution to his students. He was accordingly prosecuted by the State. The American Civil Liberties Union paid for Scopes' defence, and engaged a famous lawyer, Clarence Darrow, as his chief attorney. The State engaged an equally brilliant lawyer, W. J. Bryan, to lead for the prosecution. The case attracted nationwide interest and lasted eleven days. From a legal point of view the case, although a sensation, proved a disappointment, because the judge ruled:

(i) That there could be no argument as to whether or not the State of Tennessee had a right to pass such a law.

(ii) The question whether or not the Darwinian theory of evolution was scientifically correct, was not open to debate in the court.

(iii) The only question which could be considered by the court was whether or not Scopes had actually broken the law as laid down by the State.

Since Scopes freely admitted that he had broken the law, and since the only question at stake was whether or not an American State could pass and enforce such a law, the case ought really to have ended quite quickly and unremarkably. But Bryan very unwisely allowed himself to be put on to the witness-stand to give evidence about his own religious beliefs. This gave Darrow the chance to cross-examine him and to show up all the differences between the religious beliefs of the prosecuting attorney and the religious beliefs that lay behind the anti-evolution law. Darrow quickly made it obvious that no intelligent man, no matter how religious, could uphold in all seriousness the biblical version of creation. As a result, Bryan was made to look utterly ridiculous in a case which the entire nation was following with rapt interest. Five days later, Bryan died.

The trial ended with Scopes being found guilty, and being fined 100 dollars. He appealed to the Supreme Court of the State of Tennessee and that Court very neatly side-tracked the whole issue by acquitting Scopes on a minor technicality.

The fundamental issue—could a State pass and enforce such a law?—remained unanswered. However, in April 1967 the Tennessee House of Representatives repealed the Act of 1925. Two days later, before the repeal had been approved by the Upper Chamber and by the Governor, the School Board of a remote country area of Tennessee dismissed a biology teacher for teaching the theory of evolution.

For improvisation: imagine that such a law was passed in your own country and that a teacher in your own school fell foul of authority in the way Scopes did. Improvise a similar court case—this time allowing the two issues to be debated which were forbidden in the Scopes trial: Is it within the power of the legislature to pass such a law?

Is it possible to prove conclusively the superiority of the Darwinian theory to the biblical account?

Before improvising consider carefully the different kinds of person who might be called to give evidence, and the nature of the arguments they would employ. Take a look at the play by Lee and Lawrence: *Inherit the Wind*, which is based upon the Scopes case.

Banned Books

Great objection has been taken at various times to many books which now seem completely harmless to us—such as Flaubert, Dreiser, and D. H. Lawrence. Find a book which you consider completely, and un-questionably, harmless—a Louisa M. Alcott, perhaps, or a Harriet Beecher Stowe—read the book through very carefully, and then

37

build up a case for having it banned from the shelves of your local or school library.

Improvise a special meeting of the school or town council at which you call witnesses to testify to the evil influence which the book tends to exert. Organise the defence and the prosecution very carefully. Then try the same improvisation using a book which could more easily be held to exercise a corrupting influence of one kind or another.

(iii) A group of law cases

This particular section is not designed for the usual kind of improvisation. Nor are these cases suitable for improvising mock-trials. (For a mock-trial, turn to Section III.) This section is designed to interest the improviser in an aspect of the law that most of us never think about—arguing the law as opposed to arguing about the facts of a case. So the improvisations will be improvised debate as opposed to improvised drama. At the same time there is no reason why the situations contained in the facts of each case should not be used as a basis for improvisation if they prove sufficiently intriguing.

If at all possible, go along to a law court. Even the humblest law court—the Magistrate's Court—is fascinating. Study the way in which lawyers present their arguments and marshal their facts.

A NOTE ON ENGLISH LAW

Most of us imagine that judges and barristers spend all their time in law courts arguing over and uncovering facts. Quite often the facts are never in dispute, they are agreed upon by both sides, and what is in dispute is how the law is to be applied to the particular facts. For example, it may be freely agreed that Mr Smith the prisoner struck the blow that killed the deceased, but it may be bitterly disputed whether or not the various circumstances under which the killing took place make it murder, or manslaughter, or indeed, accidental death. In reaching decisions in such cases, the judges must follow the law of the land, but there is of course no single book to which the judges can refer to discover what the law actually is. The law is embodied in Acts of Parliament and in the cases already decided by the courts. And the task of understanding how the law applies to a new case can be an immensely complicated one. By way of illustration, have a look at the following cases.

38

In all these cases, most of which are quite recent, the facts were not in dispute. But the law was very much in dispute.

In each case, improvise a meeting of the Court of Criminal Appeal to consider the case and the application of the law to its facts. When an appeal court considers a case, it does not review the entire case, for the case itself has already been tried and judged upon. The Appeal Court merely considers the particular aspect of the case which is the subject of the appeal. Sometimes a convicted prisoner may appeal against the length of his sentence, or against the way in which the Judge at his trial summed up the evidence, or the way in which the Judge interpreted the law to the jury. All these cases fall into the last category. They are disputes as to whether or not the first court had correctly interpreted the law. Thus the prisoner himself will not be called, nor will any witnesses. For the evidence itself is not in question. Nothing more dramatic will happen than the barrister for the defence and the barrister for the prosecution presenting their legal arguments, and the judges (usually three in number) then each delivering judgment, the final decision being reached by majority vote.

Improvise the speeches of the two barristers and then the speeches of the three judges. Often all three judgments agree, but not always so, and they frequently deliver separate judgments even when they agree. The judgments should set out (*a*) the facts of the case, (*b*) how the judge understands the law to apply to the case. Obviously only a qualified lawyer could improvise a judgment that was actually based upon a true knowledge of the law, but it is a good exercise to take a court case and then attempt to judge it according to your own ideas of common sense and intelligence. Then compare your verdicts with the results actually recorded in the cases.

The verdicts in each case are given after the last case.

R v Thurborn 1849

Charge
> Larceny

Facts
> The accused found a banknote on the highway, and since there
> was no indication as to who owned the note, he decided to keep

39

it for himself. The following day, he received information from which he could easily have deduced who the true owner was, but he nevertheless kept the note and used it for himself. He was convicted of larceny.

The Appeal

The accused lodged an appeal on the grounds that the offence of stealing (larceny) can only be committed if the goods in question do definitely appear to have an owner and if the accused removes them against the will of the owner. According to this argument a person is guilty of stealing if he picks up goods in a public place under circumstances where the owner obviously knows where the goods are and will eventually come to collect them, or where the accused could reasonably be expected to know who the owner is. But he is not guilty of stealing if he picks up goods that are manifestly lost and whose owner cannot reasonably be traced. The prosecution maintained that even if the accused was not guilty of stealing at the moment of finding the note, he became guilty as soon as he learnt of the possible identity of the owner.

Improvise the appeal and judgments.

R v Ashwell 1885

Charge

Larceny

Facts

The accused asked a friend to lend him a shilling and the friend accordingly lent him a coin which at the time both believed to be a shilling. Some time later the accused discovered that the coin was in fact a sovereign, but instead of notifying the owner he kept the coin for his own use. He was later charged with and found guilty of larceny.

The Appeal

The accused appealed against his conviction on the grounds that the coin was given to him by its owner, and that at the moment of receiving it he had no intention of depriving the owner of anything. If the accused's intentions were innocent at the moment of gaining possession, then any later intentions could not change the act into larceny. The Prosecution argued that the owner of the sovereign never intended to part with its possession, and the fact that the accused formed the intention of stealing as soon as he realised the mistake that had been made, did indeed make him guilty of stealing.

Improvise the arguments and judgments.

R v Ridley 1930

Charge
    Murder
Facts
    Ridley and his colleague Betts were both found guilty of murder. Together they had devised a plan for attacking the deceased while he was on his way to the bank with some money; in executing the plan, Betts struck the deceased over the head with such violence that he killed him. At the time, Ridley was waiting in the car in which both prisoners then drove away.
The Appeal
    Ridley appealed against his conviction on the ground that he had never consented to the use of such violence as was in fact employed to strike down the deceased, and that he accordingly was not guilty of murder, though possibly guilty of manslaughter. The Prosecution argued that the accused had consented to the use of violence of one kind or another, and that this alone was sufficient to make him an accessory to the murder even though he may not have consented expressly to such violence as was actually used.

Improvise the appeal and the judgments.

R v Bentley 1952

Charge
    Murder
Facts
    Two youths, Bentley and Craig, were charged with the murder of a policeman who had been trying to arrest them on a robbery charge. At the actual moment of the murder Bentley was under arrest but called out to Craig, who had a gun, to 'let him have it' —meaning presumably to shoot the policeman, though it has

been maintained subsequently that he may have meant that Craig should hand the gun over to the police in a peaceful fashion. Craig thereupon shot the policeman dead. Both were found guilty of murder. At that time capital punishment was still employed in the United Kingdom, but Craig being younger than eighteen could not be hanged. Bentley was just within the statutory age and was accordingly sentenced to death.

The Appeal

Bentley appealed against conviction on the grounds that at the time of the murder he was under arrest and therefore could not have aided and abetted the commission of the crime. It was also argued that it was Craig who killed the policeman, not himself, and that there was no evidence of Bentley having aided and abetted Craig to commit the murder. This case created a sensation at the time, and Bentley's predicament has been hotly debated ever since.

Improvise the appeal.

Joyce v Director of Public Prosecutions 1946

Charge

High Treason

Facts

The accused was born in America, spent most of his youth in Ireland, and in 1933 obtained a British passport by making a false declaration that he was a British subject by birth. He had his passport renewed for one year in both 1938 and 1939, and in the latter year he went to Germany, declared his support for the Hitler régime, and was employed on German radio to broadcast propaganda on behalf of the enemy. Under the name of 'Lord Haw-Haw' he became a notorious legend of the Second World War. At the end of the war he was arrested in Berlin by Intelligence Officers and was brought back to England to be tried for treason. It had been widely believed throughout the War that Joyce was genuinely British—he had lived many years in England and had a British passport. When it was discovered that he was not in fact British it was widely doubted whether he could be held guilty of treason. Joyce was the object, quite rightly, of immense hatred: throughout the war his voice had constantly been heard over the radio, gloating over the news of Allied defeats and German victories, and warning of greater disasters to come. There arose the irritating question—if Joyce was not after all British, and could not be convicted of treason, then who, legally, could punish him? The possibility of his being brought before an American court was remote, as the true facts of Joyce's birth were most inaccessible, and there was equally little chance of his being brought before an international court. After a long trial, it was held that Joyce was guilty of treason even though he was not a British subject.

The Appeal

Joyce appealed on the ground that the mere holding of a passport did not of itself make him a British subject, especially as it had been obtained by making a false declaration. Therefore, since he was not British he could not be guilty of treason against the King and Country, since it was not his country or his king. The Prosecution replied that because Joyce held a British passport for the first year of the war, during which time he had already started his broadcasts for Germany, he therefore enjoyed for that time all the rights and privileges which the British government owes to any holder of a British passport. The mere fact that he had obtained the passport fraudulently did not stop him enjoying such rights and privileges. In return therefore he owed certain duties. This in effect placed him in the same position as a British subject in so far as the law of treason was concerned, and hence he could commit treason just as if he were a British subject.

Improvise the appeal.

Verdicts Recorded by the Appeal Courts:

R v Thurborn

Appeal successful. Held, that a person who keeps something that he finds is not guilty of larceny unless he believes that the owner can be discovered by taking reasonable steps.

R v Ashwell

The Appeal Court (Court for Crown Cases Reserved) was unable to reach a definite conclusion—an even number of judges were sitting and they were evenly divided on the issue—and the appeal therefore was held to fail.

R v Ridley

Appeal failed. Ridley held to be fully responsible with his partner for the murder of the deceased.

R v Bentley

Appeal failed. Bentley held to be fully responsible with his partner for the murder of the policeman.

Joyce v D.P.P.

Appeal failed. Held, that although the accused was an alien, the passport conferred upon him the protection of the Crown, and likewise conferred on him a duty of allegiance to the Crown.

If you are interested in considering more actual court cases and the way in which the law is applied, you should obtain copies of any collection of criminal cases for example:

Cases on Criminal Law by Cross and Jones
Leading Cases Illustrating the Criminal Law by A. M. Wilshere

(iv) Incidents in plays, operas and ballets

Commedia dell'Arte

This is the name given to a style of comic acting which was popular in Europe in the sixteenth to eighteenth centuries, and which originated in Italy. The players performed in travelling companies and used no written script, but mimed and improvised around various basic themes. The distinctive feature of the *Commedia dell'Arte* was that although they improvised they always used the same characters. Each actor had his own character and each character had his own particular mask and costume. The plots varied, but they all revolved around the same basic situation:

Two young people are in love with each other but cannot marry because their parents object on financial grounds. Assisted by the servants of both pairs of parents they wage a battle of wits against the parental opposition and eventually win.

The plays were broad farce, and much use was made of local dialect. Their humour often became too broad to be officially tolerated, and many of the *dell'Arte* companies were banned from reappearing in some cities because of the alleged obscenity of their jokes. But at its best the *dell'Arte* produced some of the finest improvised comedy in theatre history, and their style of humour can still be seen in the traditional circus clown, traditional pantomime, and in the silent comedies made in Hollywood in the early years of this century.

The principal characters were:

Pantaloon one of the parents or guardians; miserly, old, and hook-nosed. He loved the sound of his own voice and was always delivering long-winded advice to everyone, or else going off into extravagant flights of fury and reprimand.

Dr Grazione similar to Pantaloon, but even more exaggerated. He was parent or guardian to the other lover. More gullible than Pantaloon, he found himself saying many things the wrong way round and was full of malapropisms. He was a burlesque of the professional man—doctor or lawyer. Both Grazione and Pantaloon were extremely fond of the ladies and were convinced that all ladies, even the youngest, found them irresistible.

Capitano (The Captain) a swaggering Spaniard, who never stopped twirling his moustache and bragging of his daring deeds as a warrior. He was in fact a complete coward.

The Servants: Punch and Harlequin
There were numerous servant characters, but these were two of the most popular. The servants were shrewd, witty and impudent, and full of unexpected disguises and ingenious plans.

The Lovers
These were straight characters and did not wear masks or exaggerated costumes. The lady was usually named Colombine, the man had a wider variety of names—Florimund was one of them.

For improvisation carry out some research into the *Commedia dell' Arte*, and then create some improvised drama using the principal characters. You might use the following story as a basis on which to work: Colombine and Florimund have fallen in love but they cannot marry because Colombine's father, Pantaloon, wants her to marry the braggard Capitano who claims that he has won a vast fortune in prize money from fighting pirates on the high seas. In fact, Capitano is penniless, and has never even seen the sea, but by an intricate web of lies he manages to convince everyone of his great wealth and daring. Pantaloon sends his servant Punch to ask Dr Grazione the lawyer to come to his house and draw up the marriage contract. Dr Grazione also happens to be the father of Florimund, who always attends his father when he is on business as he is himself training to become a lawyer. Although both the parents realise that their children are in love they do not know with whom they are in love with, Grazione hopes that Florimund will marry the aged daughter of a local judge.

Punch arrives at the Grazione household to discuss the matter with Harlequin, Florimund's servant.

Work out a possible development of the plot, and then try to improvise a single scene.

The Barber of Seville

The plot of this famous opera is taken from a *Commedia dell'Arte* situation very similar to the one we have just been discussing. The handsome Count Almaviva is in love with the beautiful Rosina, who is the ward of the greedy Dr Bartolo. This unpleasant gentleman is determined that he himself will marry Rosina because she will inherit a vast sum of money on her marriage. Bartolo therefore keeps her locked up in his house and never allows her to leave the house or anyone else to come into the house to see her. The one exception is her music teacher, Don Basilio, who comes once a week to give Rosina her singing lesson. Almaviva discusses the situation with Figaro, the local barber, who proposes an ingenious plan for allowing the two lovers to meet. Figaro arranges for Don Basilio to be called away on business and then disguises Almaviva as a poor music teacher who calls round at Dr Bartolo's house to give Rosina her singing lesson in Don Basilio's place, who, he says, is very sick. The plan works but Dr Bartolo wisely insists on being present throughout the music lesson, and in order not to waste time sends for Figaro to give him a shave while the lesson is in progress. The two lovers go through the motions of a singing lesson while Figaro shaves Bartolo, and Figaro smothers the Doctor with lather whenever he begins to become suspicious. Rosina and Almaviva have arranged to elope together the next evening when suddenly the door opens and in walks Don Basilio. . . .

Improvise the story up to and beyond this point.

The Tales of Hoffmann

One night at the inn, Hoffmann, who is in a rather sad mood, tells his friends the tales of his three loves. The first is the tale of his love for Olympia. This lady was extremely beautiful and it was, on his part, a simple case of love at first sight. In fact, Olympia, whom at first he saw only through a window, was only a doll created by two sinister doctors, Coppélius and Spallanzani. In order to be near Olympia (whom he believes to be their ward) Hoffmann becomes the pupil of the two doctors and hopes in this way to be allowed eventually to meet Olympia. The doctors are well aware of Hoffmann's secret intentions but continue to encourage him because they are in need of the money that they get from him for the lessons. Eventually, at a great party, they bring on the life-size Olympia, at the same time giving Hoffmann a special pair of glasses through which the doll appears to be completely lifelike. Hoffmann is entranced with the doll and dances and sings with her, but suddenly the two doctors, in the midst of a violent quarrel over money, smash the doll in a fit of temper. His romance suddenly shattered and made ridiculous, Hoffmann runs away.

Improvise the scene in the inn with Hoffmann telling the story. Then invent the other two stories of his loves. Perhaps have all the friends around the inn table tell a story to match Hoffmann's.

La Fille Mal Gardée

In this ballet, the beautiful Lise, daughter of the rich widow Simone, is in love with a young farmer named Colas. The widow intends her daughter to marry Alain, the somewhat simple and rustic son of Thomas, a prosperous vineyard owner. Thomas comes round with Alain to make a formal proposal of marriage, also bringing with him a lawyer to draw up the marriage contract. After Simone and Thomas have discussed all the business details Thomas tells his son

47

to propose to Lise. In the ballet, Alain performs a coy and clumsy dance for Lise's benefit, which of course completely fails to win her to his side.

Improvise Alain's attempt to woo Lise, first as a mime and then as a spoken improvisation.

The Lesson

Think of the most difficult principle, practical or theoretical, that you have ever learnt—whether it be the art of mending a bicycle puncture, or Einstein's theory of relativity—and then choose a person who knows nothing whatsoever about that particular subject and endeavour to teach the principle to him. Be as patient and resourceful about it as you possibly can. Then read Ionesco's one-act play, *The Lesson*.

Everyman

In the famous medieval morality play *Everyman*, the central character learns that he is about to die, and he is told by Death that he must prepare at once to appear before God and to deliver an account of himself. He is told that he may bring with him anything that he thinks God will be favourably impressed by. Everyman calls upon Goods, Fellowship, Kindred, Discretion, Strength and Beauty to come with him but all desert him. Only Good-Deeds, assisted by Knowledge, stay by him.

Improvise Everyman's attempt to gather evidence of his worth to present to God. Imagine that he is given twenty-four hours in which to gather witnesses who will come and testify on his behalf. If you prefer, instead of using personifications such as Strength, Beauty, let Everyman go to real people he has known and lived and worked with.

II

Improvisations based on excerpts from stories, novels and plays

II Improvisations based on excerpts from stories, novels and plays

Introductory note

The group read the extract through and then discuss the story, the characters and anything of interest in the situation itself or in the way in which it is written. They then use the text as a basis for improvisation—they can if they choose, simply re-enact the scene as it is written; or take the basic situation and re-interpret it with different characters and in a totally different setting; or they may begin their improvisation at the very point where the extract leaves off. Sometimes it is a good idea if each group agrees beforehand to use a different framework for their improvisation and eventually each group can then show to the others a variation on the same theme. The purpose of the text is to provide a basic stimulus from which the group improvises something of its own—it may perhaps be a burlesque of the style of the original, or an account of what would in all probability happen in real life instead of in the pages of fiction, or of what would happen in modern Liverpool in contrast with what appears to have happened in Georgian Bath. The text gives you something to work on. The improvisation is your own.

Not all of the extracts are expected to be of equal interest to all groups. They are chosen with the aim of covering a very wide range of interests. But when a group has done a great deal of improvising it may be a good idea to return to the extracts that were at first rejected.

Some of the extracts are complete in themselves. Others finish at the very point where they become most interesting.

The Convict

from *Great Expectations* by Charles Dickens

Ours was the marsh country, down by the river, within, as the river wound, twenty miles of the sea. My first most vivid and broad impression of the identity of things, seems to me to have been gained on a memorable raw afternoon towards evening. At such a time I found out for certain, that this bleak place overgrown with nettles was the churchyard; and that Philip Pirrip, late of this parish, and also Georgiana wife of the above, were dead and buried; and that Alexander, Bartholomew, Abraham, Tobias, and Roger, infant children of the aforesaid, were also dead and buried; and that the dark flat wilderness beyond the churchyard, intersected with dykes and mounds and gates, with scattered cattle feeding on it, was the marshes; and that the low leaden line beyond was the river; and that the distant savage lair from which the wind was rushing, was the sea; and that the small bundle of shivers growing afraid of it all and beginning to cry, was Pip.

'Hold your noise!' cried a terrible voice, as a man started up from among the graves at the side of the church porch. 'Keep still, you little devil, or I'll cut your throat!'

A fearful man, all in coarse grey, with a great iron on his leg. A man with no hat, and with broken shoes, and with an old rag tied round his head. A man who had been soaked in water, and smothered in mud, and lamed by stones, and cut by flints, and stung by nettles, and torn by briars; who limped, and shivered, and glared and growled; and whose teeth chattered in his head as he seized me by the chin.

'Oh! Don't cut my throat, sir,' I pleaded in terror. 'Pray don't do it, sir.'

'Tell us your name!' said the man. 'Quick!'

'Pip, sir.'

'Once more,' said the man, staring at me. 'Give it mouth!'

'Pip. Pip, sir.'

'Show us where you live,' said the man. 'Pint out the place!'

I pointed to where our village lay, on the flat in-shore among the alder-trees and pollards, a mile or more from the church.

The man, after looking at me for a moment, turned me upside down, and emptied my pockets. There was nothing in them but a piece of bread. When the church came to itself—for he was so sudden and strong that he made it go head over heels before me, and I saw the steeple under my feet—when the church came to itself, I say, I was seated on a high tombstone, trembling, while he ate the bread ravenously.

'You young dog,' said the man, licking his lips, 'what fat cheeks you ha' got.'

I believe they were fat, though I was at that time undersized, for my years, and not strong.

'Darn me if I couldn't eat 'em,' said the man, with a threatening shake of his head, 'and if I han't half a mind to't!'

I earnestly expressed my hope that he wouldn't, and held tighter to the tombstone on which he had put me; partly, to keep myself upon it; partly, to keep myself from crying.

'Now lookee here!' said the man. 'Where's your mother?'

'There, sir!' said I.

He started, made a short run, and stopped and looked over his shoulder.

'There, sir!' I timidly explained. 'Also Georgiana. That's my mother.'

'Oh!' said he, coming back. 'And is that your father alonger your mother?'

'Yes, sir,' said I; 'him too; late of this parish.'

'Ha!' he muttered then, considering. 'Who d'ye live with—supposin' you're kindly let to live, which I han't made up my mind about?'

'My sister, sir—Mrs Joe Gargery—wife of Joe Gargery, the black-smith, sir.'

'Blacksmith. eh?' said he. And looked down at his leg.

After darkly looking at his leg and at me several times, he came closer to my tombstone, took me by both arms, and tilted me back as far as he could hold me; so that his eyes looked most powerfully down into mine, and mine looked most helplessly up into his.

'Now, lookee here,' he said, 'the question being whether you're to be let to live. You know what a file is?'

'Yes, sir.'

'And you know what wittles is?'

'Yes, sir.'

After each question he tilted me over a little more, so as to give me a greater sense of helplessness and danger.

'You get me a file.' He tilted me again. 'And you get me wittles.' He tilted me again. 'You bring 'em both to me.' He tilted me again. 'Or I'll have your heart and liver out.' He tilted me again.

I was dreadfully frightened, and so giddy that I clung to him with both hands, and said, 'If you would kindly please to let me keep upright, sir, perhaps I shouldn't be sick, and perhaps I could attend more.'

He gave me a most tremendous dip and roll, so that the church jumped over its own weather-cock. Then, he held me by the arms in an upright position on the top of the stone, and went on in these fearful terms:—

'You bring me, to-morrow morning, early, that file and them wittles. You bring the lot to me, at that old Battery over yonder. You do it, and you never dare to say a word or dare to make a sign concerning your having seen such a person as me, or any person sumever, and you shall be let to live. You fail, or you go from my words in any partickler, no matter how small it is, and your heart and your liver shall be tore out, roasted and ate. Now, I ain't alone, as you may think I am. There's a young man hid with me, in comparison with which young man I am a Angel. That young man hears the words I speak. That young man has a secret way pecooliar to himself, of getting at a boy, and at his heart, and at his liver. It is in wain for a boy to attempt to hide himself from that young man. A boy may lock his door, may be warm in his bed, may tuck himself up, may draw the clothes over his head, may think himself comfortable and safe, but that young man will softly creep and creep his way to him and tear him open. I am a keeping that young man from harming of you at the present moment, with great difficulty. I find it wery hard to hold that young man off of your inside. Now, what do you say?'

I said that I would get him the file, and I would get him what broken bits of food I could, and I would come to him at the Battery, early in the morning.

'Say, Lord strike you dead if you don't!' said the man.

I said so, and he took me down.

'Now,' he pursued, 'you remember what you've undertook, and you remember that young man, and you get home.'

'Goo-good-night, sir,' I faltered.

'Much of that!' said he, glancing about him over the cold wet flat. 'I wish I was a frog. Or a eel!'

At the same time, he hugged his shuddering body in both his arms—clasping himself, as if to hold himself together—and limped towards the low church wall. As I saw him go, picking his way among the nettles, and among the brambles that bound the green mounds, he looked in my young eyes as if he were eluding the hand of the dead people, stretching up cautiously out of their graves, to get a twist upon his ankle and pull him in.

When he came to the low church wall, he got over it, like a man whose legs were numbed and stiff, and then turned round to look for me. When I saw him turning, I set my face towards home, and made the best use of my legs. But presently I looked over my shoulder, and saw him going on again towards the river, still hugging himself in both arms, and picking his way with his sore feet among the great stones dropped into the marshes here and there, for stepping-places when the rains were heavy, or the tide was in.

Thinking of Shipping

from *Moby Dick* by Herman Melville

'Is this the Captain of the *Pequod*?' said I, advancing to the door of the tent.

'Supposing it be the Captain of the *Pequod*, what dost thou want of him?' he demanded.

'I was thinking of shipping.'

'Thou wast, wast thou? I see thou art no Nantucketer—ever been in a stove boat?'

'No, sir, I never have.'

'Dost know nothing at all about whaling, I dare say—eh?'

'Nothing sir; but I have no doubt I shall soon learn. I've been several voyages in the merchant service, and I think that——'

'Marchant service be damned. Talk not that lingo to me. Dost see that leg?—I'll take that leg away from thy stern, if ever thou talkest of the marchant service to me again. Marchant service indeed! I suppose now ye feel considerable proud of having served in those marchant ships. But flukes! Man, what makes thee want to go a-whaling, eh?—it looks a little suspicious, don't it, eh?—Hast not been a pirate, hast thou?—Didst not rob thy last Captain, didst thou? —Dost think of murdering the officers when thou gettest to sea?'

I protested my innocence of these things. I saw that under the mask of these half humorous innuendoes, this old seaman, as an insulated Quakerish Nantucketer, was full of his insular prejudices, and rather distrustful of all aliens, unless they hailed from Cape Cod or the Vineyard.

'But what takes thee a-whaling? I want to know that before I think of shipping ye.'

'Well, sir, I want to see what whaling is. I want to see the world.'

'Want to see what whaling is, eh? Have ye clapped eye on Captain Ahab?'

'Who is Captain Ahab, sir?'

'Aye, aye, I thought so. Captain Ahab is the Captain of this ship.'

'I am mistaken then. I thought I was speaking to the Captain himself.'

'Thou art speaking to Captain Peleg—that's who ye are speaking to, young man. It belongs to me and Captain Bildad to see the *Pequod* fitted out for the voyage, and supplied with all her needs, including crew. We are part owners and agents. But as I was going to say, if thou wantest to know what whaling is, as thou tellest ye do, I can put ye in a way of finding it out before ye bind yourself to it, past backing out. Clap eye on Captain Ahab, young man, and thou wilt find that he has only one leg.'

'What do you mean, sir? Was the other one lost by a whale?'

'Lost by a whale! Young man, come nearer to me: it was devoured, chewed up, crunched by the monstrousest parmacetty, that ever chipped a boat!—ah, ah!'

I was a little alarmed by his energy, perhaps also a little touched at the hearty grief in his concluding exclamation, but said as calmly as I could, 'What you say is no doubt true enough, sir; but how could I know there was any peculiar ferocity in that particular whale, though indeed I might have inferred as much from the simple fact of the accident.'

'Look ye now, young man, thy lungs are a sort of soft, d'ye see; thou dost not talk shark a bit. *Sure*, ye've been to sea before now; sure of that?'

'Sir,' said I, 'I thought I told you that I had been four voyages in the merchant——'

'Hard down out of that! Mind what I said about the marchant service—don't aggravate me—I won't have it. But let us understand each other. I have given thee a hint about what whaling is; do ye yet feel inclined for it?'

'I do, sir.'

'Very good. Now, art thou the man to pitch a harpoon down a live whale's throat, and then jump after it? Answer, quick!'

'I am, sir, if it should be positively indispensable to do so.'

'Good again. Now then, thou not only wantest to go a-whaling, to find out by experience what whaling is, but ye also want to go in order to see the world? Wast not that what ye said! I thought so. Well then, just step forward there, and take a peep over the weather-bow, and then back to me and tell me what ye see there.'

For a moment I stood a little puzzled by this curious request, not knowing exactly how to take it, whether humorously or in earnest. But concentrating all his crow's feet into one scowl, Captain Peleg started me on the errand.

Going forward and glancing over the weather-bow, I perceived that the ship swinging to her anchor with the flood-tide was now obliquely pointing towards the open ocean. The prospect was unlimited, but exceedingly monotonous and forbidding; not the slightest variety that I could see.

'Well, what's the report?' said Peleg when I came back; 'what did ye see?'

'Not much,' I replied—'nothing but water; considerable horizon though, and there's a squall coming up, I think.'

'Well, what dost thou think then of seeing the world? Do ye wish to go round Cape Horn to see any more of it, eh? Can't ye see the world where you stand?'

I was a little staggered, but go a-whaling I must, and I would; and the *Pequod* was as good a ship as any—I thought the best—and all this I now repeated to Peleg. Seeing me so determined, he expressed his willingness to ship me.

'And thou mayest as well sign the papers right off,' he added— 'come along with ye.' And so saying, he led the way below deck into the cabin.

Heartache

from *Good Wives* by Louisa M. Alcott

Something in his resolute tone made Jo look up quickly to find him looking down at her with an expression that assured her the dreaded moment had come, and made her put out her hand with an imploring:

'No, Teddy, please don't.'

'I will, and you must hear me. It's no use, Jo; we've got to have it out, and the sooner the better for both of us,' he answered, getting flushed and excited all at once.

'Say what you like then; I'll listen,' said Jo, with a desperate sort of patience.

Laurie was a young lover, but he was in earnest and meant to 'have it out', if he died in the attempt; so he plunged into the subject with characteristic impetuosity, saying in a voice that would get choky now and then, in spite of manful efforts to keep it steady:

'I've loved you ever since I've known you, Jo; couldn't help it, you've been so good to me. I've tried to show it, but you wouldn't let me; now I'm going to make you hear, and give me an answer, for I can't go on so any longer.'

'I wanted to save you this; I thought you'd understand——' began Jo, finding it a great deal harder than she expected.

'I know you did; but girls are so queer you never know what they mean. They say No when they mean Yes and drive a man out of his wits just for the fun of it,' returned Laurie, entrenching himself behind an undeniable fact.

'*I* don't. I never wanted to make you care for me so, and I went away to keep you from it if I could.'

'I thought so; it was like you, but it was no use. I only loved you all the more, and I worked hard to please you, and I gave up billiards and everything you didn't like, and waited and never complained, for I hoped you'd love me, though I'm not half good enough——' Here there was a choke that couldn't be controlled, so he decapitated buttercups while he cleared his 'confounded throat'.

'Yes, you are; you're a great deal too good for me, and I'm so grateful to you, and so proud and fond of you, I can't see why I can't love you as you want me to. I've tried but I can't change the feeling, and it would be a lie to say I do when I don't.'

'Really, truly, Jo?'

He stopped short, and caught both her hands as he put his question with a look that she did not soon forget.

'Really, truly, dear.'

They were in the grove now, close by the stile; and when the last words fell reluctantly from Jo's lips, Laurie dropped her hands and turned as if to go on, but for once in his life that fence was too much for him; so he just laid his head down on the mossy post, and stood so still that Jo was frightened.

'O Teddy, I'm so sorry, so desperately sorry, I could kill myself if it would do any good. I wish you wouldn't take it so hard. I can't help it; you know it's impossible for people to make themselves love other people if they don't,' cried Jo inelegantly but remorsefully, as she patted his shoulder, remembering the time when he had comforted her so long ago.

'They do sometimes,' said a muffled voice from the post.

'I don't believe it's the right sort of love, and I'd rather not try it,' was the decided answer.

There was a long pause, while a blackbird sung blithely on the willow by the river, and the tall grass rustled in the wind. Presently Jo said, very soberly, as she sat down on the step of the stile:

'Laurie, I want to tell you something.'

He started as if he had been shot, threw up his head, and cried out in a fierce tone:

'Don't tell me that, Jo; I can't bear it now.'

'Tell what?' she asked, wondering at his violence.

'That you love that old man.'

'What old man?' demanded Jo, thinking he must mean his grandfather.

'That devilish Professor you were always writing about. If you say you love him, I know I shall do something desperate.' And he looked as if he would keep his word, as he clenched his hands with a wrathful spark in his eyes.

Jo wanted to laugh, but restrained herself, and said warmly, for she, too, was getting excited with all this:

'Don't swear, Teddy. He isn't old, nor anything bad, but good and kind, and the best friend I've got next to you. Pray don't fly into a passion; I want to be kind, but I know I shall get angry if you abuse my Professor. I haven't the least idea of loving him or anybody else.'

'But you will after a while, and then what will become of me?'

'You'll love someone else too, like a sensible boy, and forget all this trouble.'

'I can't love any one else; and I'll never forget you, Jo, never, never!' with a stamp to emphasise his passionate words.

'I agree with mother that you and I are not suited to each other, because our quick tempers and strong wills would probably make us very miserable, if we were so foolish as to——' Jo paused a little over the last word, but Laurie uttered with a rapturous expression:

'Marry—no, we shouldn't. If you loved me, Jo, I should be a perfect saint, for you could make me anything you like.'

'No, I can't. I've tried it and failed, and I won't risk our happiness by such a serious experiment. We don't agree and we never shall; so we'll be good friends all our lives, but we won't go and do anything rash.'

'Yes, we will if we get the chance,' muttered Laurie rebelliously.

'Now do be reasonable and take a sensible view of the case,' implored Jo, almost at her wit's end.

'I won't be reasonable; I don't want to take what you call a sensible view; it won't help me, and it only makes you harder. I don't believe you've got a heart.'

'I wish I hadn't.'

There was a little quiver in Jo's voice, and thinking it a good omen, Laurie turned round, bringing all his persuasive powers to bear as he said, in the wheedlesome tone that had never been so dangerously wheedlesome before:

'Don't disappoint us, dear. Everyone expects it. Grandpa has set his heart upon it, your people like it, and I can't get on without you. Say you will, and let's be happy. Do, do.'

Not until months afterwards did Jo understand how she had the strength of mind to hold fast to the resolution she had made when she decided that she did not love her boy and never could. It was very hard to do, but she did it, knowing that delay was both useless and cruel.

'I can't say "Yes" truly, so I won't say it at all. You'll see that I'm right by and by, and thank me for it——' she began solemnly.

'I'll be hanged if I do,' and Laurie bounded up off the grass, burning with indignation at the bare idea.

'Yes, you will,' persisted Jo; 'you'll get over this after a while, and find some lovely accomplished girl, who will adore you, and make a fine mistress for your fine house. I shouldn't. I'm homely and awkward and odd and old, and you'd be ashamed of me, and we would quarrel —we can't help it even now, you see—and I shouldn't like elegant society and you would, and you'd hate my scribbling, and I couldn't get on without it, and we should be unhappy and wish we hadn't done it, and everything would be horrid.'

'Anything more?' asked Laurie, finding it hard to listen patiently to this prophetic outburst.

'Nothing more, except that I don't believe I shall ever marry. I'm happy as I am, and love my liberty too well to be in any hurry to give it up for any mortal man.'

'I know better,' broke in Laurie. 'You think so now; but there'll come a time when you *will* care for somebody, and you'll love him tremendously, and live and die for him. I know you will, it's your way, and I shall have to stand by and see it.'

'Yes, I *will* live and die for him, if he ever comes and makes me love him in spite of myself, and you must do the best you can. I've done my best, but you won't be reasonable, and it's selfish of you to keep teasing for what I can't give. I shall always be fond of you, very fond indeed, as a friend, but I'll never marry you; and the sooner you believe it, the better for both of us—so now!'

That speech was like fire to gunpowder. Laurie looked at her a minute as if he did not quite know what to do with himself, then turned sharply away, saying in a desperate sort of tone:

'You'll be sorry some day, Jo.'

'Oh, where are you going?' she cried, for his face frightened her.

'To the devil!' was the consoling answer.

Frankenstein and his Creature

from *Frankenstein* by Mary Shelley

I suddenly beheld the figure of a man, at some distance, advancing towards me with superhuman speed. He bounded over the crevices in the ice, among which I had walked with caution; his stature, also, as he approached, seemed to exceed that of man. I was troubled: a mist came over my eyes, and I felt a faintness seize me; but I was quickly restored by the cold gale of the mountains. I perceived, as the shape came nearer (sight tremendous and abhorred) that it was the wretch whom I had created. I trembled with rage and horror, resolving to wait his approach, and then close with him in mortal combat. He approached; his countenance bespoke bitter anguish, combined with disdain and malignity, while its unearthly ugliness rendered it almost too horrible for human eyes. But I scarcely observed this; rage and hatred had at first deprived me of utterance, and I recovered only to overwhelm him with words expressive of furious detestation and contempt.

'Devil,' I exclaimed, 'do you dare approach me? and do not you fear the fierce vengeance of my arm wreaked on your miserable head? Begone, vile insect. Or rather stay, that I may trample you to dust, and oh that I could, with the extinction of your miserable existence, restore those victims whom you have so diabolically murdered.'

'I expected this reception,' said the daemon. 'All men hate the wretched; how then, must I be hated, who am miserable beyond all living things. Yet you, my creator, detest and spurn me, thy creature, to whom thou art bound by ties only dissoluble by the annihilation of one of us. You purpose to kill me. How dare you sport thus with life? Do your duty towards me, and I will do mine towards you and the rest of mankind. If you will comply with my conditions, I will leave them and you at peace; but if you refuse, I will glut the maw of death, until it be satiated with the blood of your remaining friends.'

'Abhorred monster, fiend thou art. The tortures of hell are too mild a vengeance for your crimes. Wretched devil. You reproach me with your creation; come on, then, that I may extinguish the spark which I so negligently bestowed.'

My rage was without bounds; I sprang on him, impelled by all the feelings which can arm one being against the existence of another.

He easily eluded me, and said—

'Be calm. I entreat you to hear me, before you give vent to your hatred on my devoted head. Have I not suffered enough that you seek to increase my misery? Life, although it may only be an accumulation of anguish, is dear to me, and I will defend it. Remember, thou hast made me more powerful than thyself; my height is superior to thine; my joints more supple. But I will not be tempted to set myself in opposition to thee. I am thy creature, and I will be even mild and docile to my natural lord and king, if thou wilt also perform thy part, the which thou owest me. Oh, Frankenstein, be not equable to every other, and trample upon me alone, to whom thy justice, and even thy clemency and affection, is most due. Remember that I am thy creature; I ought to be thy Adam; but I am rather the fallen angel, whom thou drivest from joy for no misdeed. Everywhere I see bliss, from which I alone am irrevocably excluded. I was benevolent and good; misery made me a fiend. Make me happy and I shall again be virtuous.'

'Begone. I will not hear you. There can be no community between you and me. We are enemies. Begone, or let us try our strength in a fight, in which one must fall.'

'How can I move thee? Will no entreaties cause thee to turn a favourable eye upon thy creature, who implores thy goodness and compassion? Believe me, Frankenstein: I was benevolent; my soul glowed with love and humanity: but am I not alone, miserably alone? You, my creator, abhor me; what hope can I gather from your fellow-creatures, who owe me nothing? They spurn and hate me. The desert mountains and dreary glaciers are my refuge. I have wandered here many days; the caves of ice, which I only do not fear, are a dwelling to me, and the only one which man does not grudge. These bleak skies I hail, for they are kinder to me than your fellow-beings. If the multitude of mankind knew of my existence, they would do as you do, and arm themselves for my destruction. Shall I not then hate them who abhor me? I will keep no terms with my enemies. I am miserable, and they shall share my wretchedness. Yet it is in your power to recompense me, and deliver them from an evil which it only remains for you to make so great, that not only you and your family, but thousands of others, shall be swallowed up in the whirlwinds of rage. Let your compassion be moved, and do not disdain me. Listen to my tale; when you have heard that, abandon or commiserate me, as you shall judge that I deserve. But hear me. The guilty are allowed, by human laws, bloody as they are, to speak in their own defence, before they are condemned. Listen to me, Frankenstein. You accuse me of murder; and yet you would with a satisfied conscience, destroy your own creature. Oh, praise the eternal justice of man! Yet I ask you not to spare me: listen to me; and then, if you can, and if you will, destroy the work of your hands.'

'Why do you call to my remembrance,' I rejoined, 'circumstances of which I shudder to reflect, that I have been the miserable origin and author? Cursed be the day, abhorred devil, in which you first saw light. Cursed, although I curse myself, be the hands that formed you. You have made me wretched beyond expression. You have left me no power to consider whether I am just to you or not. Begone. Relieve me from the sight of your detested form.'

'Thus I relieve thee, my creator,' he said, and placed his hated hands before my eyes, which I flung from me with violence. 'Thus I take from thee a sight which you abhor. Still thou canst listen to me, and grant me thy compassion. By the virtues that I once possessed, I demand this from you. Hear my tale; it is long and strange, and the temperature of this place is not fitting to your fine sensations; come to the hut upon the mountain. The sun is yet high in the heavens; before it descends to hide itself beyond yon snowy precipices, and illuminate another world, you will have heard my story and can decide. On you it rests whether I quit for ever the neighbourhood of man and lead a harmless life, or become the scourge of your fellow-creatures and the author of your own speedy ruin.'

As he said this, he led the way across the ice; I followed. My heart was full, and I did not answer him; but as I proceeded, I weighed the various arguments that he had used, and determined at least to listen to his tale. I was partly urged by curiosity, and compassion confirmed my resolution. I had hitherto supposed him to be the murderer of my brother, and I eagerly sought a confirmation or denial of this opinion. For the first time also, I felt what the duties of a creator towards his

63

creature were, and that I ought to render him happy before I complained of his wickedness. These motives urged me to comply with his demand. We crossed the ice, therefore, and ascended the opposite rock. The air was cold, and the rain again began to descend: we entered the hut, the fiend with an air of exultation, I with a heavy heart and depressed spirits. But I consented to listen; and seating myself by the fire which my odious companion had lighted, he thus began his tale.

The Family Conference

from *The Mill on the Floss* by George Eliot

(Financial disaster and serious illness have struck down Mr Tulliver. His wife's family gather together to debate the situation . . .)

Mrs Deane was the first to arrive; and when she had taken her seat in the large parlour, Mrs Tulliver came down to her with her comely face a little distorted, nearly as it would have been if she had been crying: she was not a woman who could shed abundant tears, except in moments when the prospect of losing her furniture became unusually vivid, but she felt how unfitting it was to be quite calm under present circumstances.

'Oh, sister, what a world this is!' she exclaimed as she entered: 'what trouble, oh dear!'

Mrs Deane was a thin-lipped woman, who made small well-considered speeches on peculiar occasions, repeating them afterwards to her husband, and asking him if she had not spoken very properly.

'Yes, sister,' she said deliberately, 'this is a changing world, and we don't know to-day what may happen to-morrow. But it's right to be prepared for all things, and if trouble's sent, to remember as it isn't sent without a cause. I'm very sorry for you as a sister, and if the doctor orders jelly for Mr Tulliver, I hope you'll let me know: I'll send it willingly. For it is but right he should have proper attendance while he's ill.'

'Thank you, Susan,' said Mrs Tulliver, rather faintly, withdrawing her fat hand from her sister's thin one. 'But there's been no talk o' jelly yet.' Then after a moment's pause she added, 'There's a dozen o' cut jelly-glasses up-stairs. . . . I shall never put jelly into 'em no more.'

Her voice was rather agitated as she uttered the last words, but the sound of wheels diverted her thoughts. Mr and Mrs Glegg were come, and were almost immediately followed by Mr and Mrs Pullet.

Mrs Pullet entered crying, as a compendious mode, at all times, of expressing what were her views of life in general, and what, in brief, were the opinions she held concerning the particular case before her.

Mrs Glegg had on her fuzziest front, and garments which appeared to have had a recent resurrection from rather a creasy form of burial; a costume selected with the high moral purpose of instilling perfect humility into Bessy and her children.

'Mrs G., won't you come nearer the fire?' said her husband, unwilling to take the more comfortable seat without offering it to her.

'You see I've seated myself here, Mr Glegg,' returned this superior woman; '*you* can roast yourself, if you like.'

'Well,' said Mr Glegg, seating himself good-humouredly, 'and how's the poor man up-stairs?'

'Dr Turnbull thought him a deal better this morning,' said Mrs Tulliver; 'he took more notice, and spoke to me; but he's never known Tom yet—looks at the poor lad as if he was a stranger, though he said something once about Tom and the pony. The doctor says his memory's gone a long way back, and he doesn't know Tom because he's thinking of him when he was little. Eh dear, eh dear!'

'I doubt it's the water got on his brain,' said aunt Pullet, turning round from adjusting her cap in a melancholy way at the pier-glass. 'It's much if he ever gets up again; and if he does, he'll most like be childish, as Mr Carr was, poor man! They fed him with a spoon as if he'd been a baby for three year. He'd quite lost the use of his limbs; but then he'd got a Bath chair, and somebody to draw him; and that's what you won't have, I doubt, Bessy.'

'Sister Pullet,' said Mrs Glegg, severely, 'if I understand right, we've come together this morning to advise and consult about what's to be done in this disgrace as has fallen upon the family, and not to talk o' people as don't belong to us. Mr Carr was none of our blood, nor noways connected with us, as I've ever heard.'

'Sister Glegg,' said Mrs Pullet, in a pleading tone, drawing on her gloves again, and stroking the fingers in an agitated manner, 'if you've got anything disrespectful to say o' Mr Carr, I do beg of you as you won't say it to me. *I* know what he was,' she added, with a sigh; 'his breath was short to that degree as you could hear him two rooms off.'

'Sophy!' said Mrs Glegg, with indignant disgust, 'you *do* talk o' people's complaints till it's quite undecent. But I say again, as I said before, I didn't come away from home to talk about acquaintance, whether they'd short breath or long. If we aren't come together for one to hear what the other 'ull do to save a sister and her children from the parish, *I* shall go back. *One* can't act without the other, I suppose, it isn't to be expected as *I* should do everything.'

'Well, Jane,' said Mrs Pullet, 'I don't see as you've been so very forrard at doing. So far as I know, this is the first time as here you've been, since it's been known as the bailiff's in the house; and I was here yesterday, and looked at all Bessy's linen and things, and I told her I'd buy in the spotted tablecloths. I couldn't speak fairer; for as for the teapot as she doesn't want to go out o' the family, it stands to sense I can't do with two silver teapots, not if it hadn't a straight spout—but the spotted damask I was allays fond on.'

'I wish it could be managed so as my teapot and chany and the best castors needn't be put up for sale,' said poor Mrs Tulliver, beseeching-ly, 'and the sugar-tongs, the first things ever I bought.'

'But that can't be helped, you know,' said Mr Glegg. 'If one o' the family chooses to buy 'em in, they can, but one thing must be bid for as well as another.'

'And it isn't to be looked for,' said uncle Pullet, with unwonted independence of idea, 'as your own family should pay more for things nor they'll fetch. They may go for an old song by auction.'

'Oh dear, oh dear,' said Mrs Tulliver, 'to think o' my chany being sold i' that way—and I bought it when I was married, just as you did yours, Jane and Sophy: and I know you didn't like mine, because o' the sprig, but I was fond of it; and there's never been a bit broke, for I've washed it myself—and there's the tulips on the cups, and the roses, as anybody might go and look at 'em for pleasure. You wouldn't like *your* chany to go for an old song and be broke to pieces, though yours 'as got no colour in it, Jane—it's all white and fluted, and didn't cost so much as mine. And there's the castors—sister Deane. I can't think but you'd like to have the castors, for I've heard you say they're pretty.'

'Well, I've no objection to buy some of the best things,' said Mrs Deane, rather loftily; 'we can do with extra things in our house.'

'Best things!' exclaimed Mrs Glegg with severity, which had gathered intensity from her long silence. 'It drives me past patience to hear you all talking o' best things, and buying in this, that, and the other, such as silver and chany. You must bring your mind to your circumstances, Bessy, and not be thinking o' silver and chany; but whether you shall get so much as a flock-bed to lie on, and a blanket to cover you, and a stool to sit on. You must remember, if you get 'em, it'll be because your friends have bought 'em for you, for you're dependent upon *them* for everything; for your husband lies there helpless, and hasn't got a penny i' the world to call his own. And it's for your own good I say this, for it's right you should feel what your state is, and what disgrace your husband's brought on your own family, as you've got to look to for everything—and be humble in your mind.'

Mrs Glegg paused, for speaking with much energy for the good of others is naturally exhausting. Mrs Tulliver, always borne down by the family predominance of sister Jane, who had made her wear the yoke of a younger sister in very tender years, said pleadingly—

'I'm sure, sister, I've never asked anybody to do anything, only buy things as it 'ud be a pleasure to 'em to have, so as they mightn't go and be spoiled i' strange houses. I never asked anybody to buy the things in for me and my children; though there's the linen I spun, and I thought when Tom was born—I thought one o' the first things when he was lying i' the cradle, as all the things I'd bought wi' my own money, and been so careful of, 'ud go to him. But I've said nothing as I wanted my sisters to pay their money for me. What my husband has done for *his* sister's unknown, and we should ha' been better off this day if it hadn't been as he's lent money and never asked for it again.'

'Come, come,' said Mr Glegg, kindly, 'don't let us make things too dark. What's done can't be undone. We shall make a shift among us to buy what's sufficient for you; though, as Mrs G. says, they must be useful, plain things. We mustn't be thinking o' what's unnecessary. A table, and a chair or two, and kitchen things, and a good bed, and suchlike. Why, I've seen the day when I shouldn't ha' known myself if I'd lain on sacking i'stead o' the floor. We get a deal o' useless things about us, only because we've got the money to spend.'

'Mr Glegg,' said Mrs G., 'if you'll be kind enough to let me speak, i'stead o' taking the words out o' my mouth—I was going to say, Bessy, as it's fine talking for you to say as you've never asked us to buy anything for you; let me tell you, you *ought* to have asked us. Pray, how are you to be purvided for, if your own family don't help you? You must go on the parish, if they didn't. And you ought to know that, and keep it in mind, and ask us humble to do what we can for you, i'stead o' saying, and making a boast, as you've never asked us for anything.'

The Murder of the King

In Shakespeare's play *Macbeth* a Scottish general is ambitious to be King. When the real King, Duncan, comes to visit him, Macbeth and his wife plan to murder him, at night while he lies sleeping. . . . The first extract is from *Tales from Shakespeare* by Charles and Mary Lamb. The second is from the play itself.

The king being tired with his journey, went early to bed, and in his state-room two grooms of his chamber (as was the custom) slept beside him. He had been unusually pleased with his reception, and had made presents before he retired to his principal officers; and among the rest, had sent a rich diamond to lady Macbeth, greeting her by the name of his most kind hostess.

Now was the middle of night, when over half the world nature seems dead, and wicked dreams abuse men's minds asleep, and none but the wolf and the murderer is abroad. This was the time when lady Macbeth waked to plot the murder of the king. She would not have undertaken a deed so abhorrent to her sex, but that she feared her husband's nature, that it was too full of the milk of human kindness, to do a contrived murder. She knew him to be ambitious, but withal to be scrupulous, and not yet prepared for that height of crime which commonly in the end accompanies inordinate ambition. She had won him to consent to the murder, but she doubted his resolution; and she feared that the natural tenderness of his disposition (more humane than her own) would come between, and defeat the purpose. So with her own hands armed with a dagger, she approached the king's bed; having taken care to ply the grooms of his chamber so with wine, that they slept intoxicated, and careless of their charge. There lay Duncan in a sound sleep after the fatigues of his journey, and as she viewed him earnestly, there was something in his face, as he slept, which resembled her own father; and she had not the courage to proceed.

She returned to confer with her husband. His resolution had begun to stagger. He considered that there were strong reasons against the deed. In the first place, he was not only a subject, but a near kinsman to the king; and he had been his host and entertainer that day, whose

68

duty, by the laws of hospitality, it was to shut the door against his murderers, not bear the knife himself. Then he considered how just and merciful a king this Duncan had been, how clear of offence to his subjects, how loving to his nobility, and in particular to him; that such kings are the peculiar care of Heaven, and their subjects doubly bound to revenge their deaths. Besides, by the favours of the king, Macbeth stood high in the opinion of all sorts of men, and how would those honours be stained by the reputation of so foul a murder!

In these conflicts of the mind lady Macbeth found her husband inclining to the better part, and resolving to proceed no further. But she being a woman not easily shaken from her evil purpose, began to pour in at his ears words which infused a portion of her own spirit into his mind, assigning reason upon reason why he should not shrink from what he had undertaken; how easy the deed was; how soon it would be over; and how the action of one short night would give to all their nights and days to come sovereign sway and royalty! Then she threw contempt on his change of purpose, and accused him of fickleness and cowardice; and declared that she had given suck, and knew how tender it was to love the babe that milked her; but she would, while it was smiling in her face, have plucked it from her breast, and dashed its brains out, if she had so sworn to do it, as he had sworn to perform that murder. Then she added, how practicable it was to lay the guilt of the deed upon the drunken sleepy grooms. And with the valour of her tongue she so chastised his sluggish resolutions, that he once more summoned up courage to the bloody business.

Enter Lady Macbeth

Macbeth   How now! what news?
Lady M. He has almost supp'd: why have you left the chamber?
Macbeth Hath he ask'd for me?
Lady M.   Know you not he has?
Macbeth We will proceed no further in this business:
  He hath honour'd me of late; and I have bought
  Golden opinions from all sorts of people,
  Which would be worn now in their newest gloss,
  Not cast aside so soon.
Lady M.   Was the hope drunk
  Wherein you dress'd yourself? hath it slept since?

And wakes it now, to look so green and pale
At what it did so freely? From this time
Such I account thy love. Art thou afeard
To be the same in thine own act and valour
As thou art in desire? Wouldst thou have that
Which thou esteem'st the ornament of life,
And live a coward in thine own esteem,
Letting 'I dare not' wait upon 'I would',
Like the poor cat i' the adage?
Macbeth   Prithee, peace:
    I dare do all that may become a man;
    Who dares do more is none.
Lady M.   What beast was't, then,
    That made you break this enterprise to me?
    When you durst do it, then you were a man;
    And, to be more than what you were, you would
    Be so much more the man. Nor time nor place
    Did then adhere, and yet you would make both:
    They have made themselves, and that their fitness now
    Does unmake you. I have given suck, and know
    How tender 'tis to love the babe that milks me:
    I would, while it was smiling in my face,
    Have pluck'd my nipple from his boneless gums,
    And dash'd the brains out, had I so sworn as you
    Have done to this.
Macbeth   If we should fail?
Lady M.   We fail!
    But screw your courage to the sticking-place,
    And we'll not fail. When Duncan is asleep—
    Whereto the rather shall his day's hard journey
    Soundly invite him—his two chamberlains
    Will I with wine and wassail so convince
    That memory, the warder of the brain,
    Shall be a fume, and the receipt of reason
    A limbeck only: when in swinish sleep
    Their drenched natures lie as in a death,
    What cannot you and I perform upon
    The unguarded Duncan? what not put upon
    His spongy officers, who shall bear the guilt
    Of our great quell?

Macbeth   Bring forth men-children only;
   For thy undaunted mettle should compose
   Nothing but males. Will it not be received,
   When we have mark'd with blood those sleepy two
   Of his own chamber and used their very daggers,
   That they have done't?
Lady M.   Who dares receive it other,
   As we shall make our griefs and clamour roar
   Upon his death?
Macbeth   I am settled, and bend up
   Each corporal agent to this terrible feat.
   Away, and mock the time with fairest show:
   False face must hide what the false heart doth know.

Exeunt

Before the Battle

from *The Red Badge of Courage* by Stephen Crane

He lay down in the grass. The blades pressed tenderly against his cheek. The moon had been lighted and was hung in a treetop. The liquid stillness of the night enveloping him made him feel vast pity for himself. There was a caress in the soft winds; and the whole mood of the darkness, he thought, was one of sympathy for himself in his distress.

He wished, without reserve, that he was at home again making the endless rounds from the house to the barn, from the barn to the fields, from the fields to the barn, from the barn to the house. He remembered he had often cursed the brindle cow and her mates, and had sometimes flung milking stools. But, from his present point of view, there was a halo of happiness about each of their heads, and he would have sacrificed all the brass buttons on the continent to have been enabled to return to them. He told himself that he was not formed for a soldier. And he mused seriously upon the radical differences between himself and those men who were dodging imp-like around the fires.

As he mused thus he heard the rustle of grass, and, upon turning his head, discovered the loud soldier. He called out, 'Oh, Wilson!'

The latter approached and looked down. 'Why, hello, Henry; is it you? What you doing here?'

71

'Oh, thinking,' said the youth.

The loud soldier launched then into the subject of the anticipated fight. 'Oh, we've got 'em now!' As he spoke his boyish face was wreathed in a gleeful smile, and his voice had an exultant ring. 'We've got 'em now. At last, by the eternal thunders, we'll lick 'em good!

'If the truth was known,' he added more soberly, '*they*'*ve* licked *us* about every clip up to now; but this time—this time—we'll lick 'em good!'

'I thought you was objecting to this march a little while ago,' said the youth coldly.

'Oh, it wasn't that,' explained the other. 'I don't mind marching, if there's going to be fighting at the end of it. What I hate is this getting moved here and moved there, with no good coming of it, as far as I can see, excepting sore feet and damned short rations.'

'Well, Jim Conklin says we'll get aplenty of fighting this time.'

'He's right for once, I guess, though I can't see how it come. This time we're in for a big battle, and we've got the best end of it, certain sure. Gee rod! how we will thump 'em!'

He arose and began to pace to and fro excitedly. The thrill of his enthusiasm made him walk with an elastic step. He was sprightly, vigorous, fiery in his belief in success. He looked into the future with clear, proud eye, and he swore with the air of an old soldier.

The youth watched him for a moment in silence. When he finally spoke his voice was as bitter as dregs. 'Oh, you're going to do great things, I s'pose!'

The loud soldier blew a thoughtful cloud of smoke from his pipe. 'Oh, I don't know,' he remarked with dignity; 'I don't know. I s'pose I'll do as well as the rest. I'm going to try like thunder.' He evidently complimented himself upon the modesty of this statement.

'How do you know you won't run when the time comes?' asked the youth.

'Run?' said the loud one; 'run?—of course not!' He laughed.

'Well,' continued the youth, 'lots of good-a-'nough men have thought they was going to do great things before the fight, but when the time come they skedaddled.'

'Oh, that's all true, I s'pose,' replied the other; 'but I'm not going to skedaddle. The man that bets on my running will lose his money, that's all.' He nodded confidently.

'Oh, shucks!' said the youth. 'You ain't the bravest man in the world, are you?'

'No, I ain't,' exclaimed the loud soldier indignantly; 'and I didn't say I was the bravest man in the world, neither. I said I was going to do my share of fighting—that's what I said. And I am, too. Who are you, anyhow? You talk as if you thought you was Napoleon Bonaparte.' He glared at the youth for a moment, and then strode away.

The youth called in a savage voice after his comrade: 'Well, you needn't git mad about it!' But the other continued on his way and made no reply.

He felt alone in space when his injured comrade had disappeared. His failure to discover any mite of resemblance in their viewpoints made him more miserable than before. No one seemed to be wrestling with such a terrific personal problem. He was a mental outcast.

He went slowly to his tent and stretched himself on a blanket by the side of the snoring tall soldier. In the darkness he saw visions of a thousand-tongued fear that would babble at his back and cause him to flee, while others were going coolly about their country's business. He admitted that he would not be able to cope with this monster. He felt that every nerve in his body would be an ear to hear the voices, while other men would remain stolid and deaf.

And as he sweated with the pain of these thoughts, he could hear low, serene sentences. 'I'll bid five.' 'Make it six.' 'Seven.' 'Seven goes.'

He stared at the red, shivering reflection of a fire on the white wall of his tent until, exhausted and ill from the monotony of his suffering, he fell asleep.

Caught in the Act

from *Tom Brown's Schooldays* by Thomas Hughes

So one fine Thursday afternoon, Tom having borrowed East's new rod, started by himself to the river. He fished for some time with small success, not a fish would rise at him; but as he prowled along the bank he was presently aware of mighty ones feeding in a pool on the opposite side, under the shade of a huge willow tree. The stream was deep here, but some fifty yards below was a shallow, for which he made off hotfoot; and forgetting landlords, keepers, solemn prohibitions of the Doctor, and everything else, pulled up his trousers, plunged across, and in three minutes was creeping along on all-fours towards the clump of willows.

It isn't often that great chub, or any other coarse fish, are in earnest about anything, but just then they were thoroughly bent on feeding, and in half an hour Master Tom had deposited three thumping fellows at the foot of the giant willow. As he was baiting for a fourth pounder, and just going to throw in again, he became aware of a man coming up the bank not one hundred yards off. Another look told him that it was the underkeeper. Could he reach the shallow before him? No, not carrying his rod. Nothing for it but the tree, so Tom laid his bones to it, shinning up as fast as he could, and dragging up his rod after him. He had just time to reach and crouch along upon a huge branch some ten feet up, which stretched out over the river, when the keeper arrived at the clump. Tom's heart beat fast as he came under the tree; two steps more and he would have passed, when, as ill-luck would have it, the gleam on the scales of the dead fish caught his eye, and he made a dead point at the foot of the tree. He picked up the fish one by one; his eye and touch told him that they had been alive and feeding within the hour. Tom crouched lower along the branch, and heard the keeper beating the clump. 'If I could only get the rod hidden,' thought he, and began gently shifting it to get it alongside him; 'willow trees don't throw out straight hickory shoots twelve feet long, with no leaves, worse luck.' Alas! the keeper catches the rustle, and then a sight of the rod, and then of Tom's hand and arm.

'Oh, be up ther' be 'ee?' says he, running under the tree. 'Now you come down this minute.'

'Tree'd at last,' thinks Tom, making no answer, and keeping as close as possible, but working away at the rod, which he takes to pieces; 'I'm in for it, unless I can starve him out.' And then he begins to meditate getting along the branch for a plunge, and scramble to the other side; but the small branches are so thick, and the opposite bank so difficult, that the keeper will have lots of time to get round by the ford before he can get out, so he gives that up. And now he hears the keeper beginning to scramble up the trunk. That will never do; so he scrambles himself back to where his branch joins the trunk, and stands with lifted rod.

'Hallo, Velveteens, mind your fingers if you come any higher.'

The keeper stops and looks up, and then with a grin says, 'Oh! be you, be it, young measter? Well, here's luck. Now I tells 'ee to come down at once, and 't'll be best for 'ee.'

'Thank'ee, Velveteens, I'm very comfortable,' said Tom, shortening the rod in his hand, and preparing for battle.

74

'Werry well, please yourself,' says the keeper, descending, however, to the ground again, and taking his seat on the bank; 'I bean't in no hurry, so you med' take your time. I'll larn'ee to gee honest folk names afore I've done with 'ee.'

'My luck as usual,' thinks Tom; 'what a fool I was to give him a black. If I'd called him 'keeper' now I might get off. The return match is all his way.'

The keeper quietly proceeded to take out his pipe, fill, and light it, keeping an eye on Tom, who now sat disconsolately across the branch, looking at keeper—a pitiful sight for men and fishes. The more he thought of it the less he liked it. 'It must be getting near second calling-over,' thinks he. Keeper smokes on stolidly. 'If he takes me up I shall be flogged safe enough. I can't sit here all night. Wonder if he'll rise at silver.'

'I say, keeper,' said he, meekly, 'let me go for two bob?'

'Not for twenty neither,' grunts his persecutor.

And so they sat on till long past second calling-over, and the sun came slanting in through the willow branches.

'I'm coming down, keeper,' said Tom at last with a sigh, fairly tired out. 'Now what are you going to do?'

'Walk 'ee up to School, and give 'ee over to the Doctor; them's my orders,' says Velveteen, knocking the ashes out of his fourth pipe, and standing up and shaking himself.

'Very good,' said Tom; 'but hands off, you know. I'll go with you quietly, so no collaring or that sort of thing.'

Keeper looked at him a minute—'Werry good,' said he at last; and so Tom descended, and wended his way, drearily, by the side of the keeper up to the Schoolhouse, where they arrived just at locking-up.

The Quaker Provoked

from *John Halifax, Gentleman* by Mrs Craik

'Mr Brithwood, let me introduce you to a new friend of mine.'

The squire bowed rather awkwardly; proving the truth of what Norton Bury often whispered, that Richard Brithwood was more at home with grooms than gentlemen.

'He belongs to this your town—you must have heard of him, perhaps met him.'

'I have more than once had the pleasure of meeting Mr Brithwood, but he has doubtless forgotten it.'

'By Jove! I have. What might your name be, sir?'

'John Halifax.'

'What, Halifax the tanner?'

'The same.'

'Phew!' He began a low whistle, and turned on his heel.

'*Mon ami*—you forget; I have introduced you to this gentleman.'

'Gentleman, indeed! Pooh! rubbish! Lady Caroline—I'm busy talking.'

'And so are we, most pleasantly. I only called you as a matter of form, to ratify my invitation. Mr Halifax will, I hope, dine with us next Sunday?'

'The devil he will!'

'Richard—you hurt me!'—with a little scream, as she pushed his rough fingers from her arm, so soft, and round, and fair.

The squire called across the room, in a patronizing tone: 'My good fellow—that is, ahem! I say, young Halifax?'

'Were you addressing me, Mr Brithwood?'

'I was. I want a quiet word or two—between ourselves.'

'Certainly.'

They stood face to face. The one seemed uncomfortable, the other was his natural self—a little graver, perhaps, as if he felt what was coming, and prepared to meet it, knowing in whose presence he had to prove himself—what Richard Brithwood, with all his broad acres, could never be—a gentleman.

Few could doubt that fact who looked at the two young men, as all were looking now.

'On my soul, it's awkward—I'll call at the tanyard and explain.'

'I had rather you would explain here.'

'Well, then, though it's a confounded unpleasant thing to say—and I really wish I had not been brought into such a position—you'll not heed my wife's nonsense?'

'I do not understand you.'

'Come, it's no use running to cover in that way. Let's be open and plain. I mean no offence. You may be a very respectable young man for aught I know, still rank is rank. Of course Dr Jessop asks whom he likes to his house—and, by George! I'm always civil to everybody —but really, in spite of my lady's likings, I can't well invite you to my table!'

'Nor could I humiliate myself by accepting any such invitation.'

He said the words distinctly, so that the whole circle might have heard, and was turning away, when Mr Brithwood fired up—as an angry man does in a losing game.

'Humiliate yourself! What do you mean, sir? Wouldn't you be only too thankful to crawl into the houses of your betters, anyhow, by hook or by crook? Ha! Ha! I know you would. It's always the way with you common folk, you rioters, you revolutionists. By the Lord! I wish you were all hanged.'

The young blood rose fiercely in John's cheek, but he restrained himself. 'Sir, I am neither a rioter nor a revolutionist.'

'But you are a tradesman? You used to drive Fletcher's cart of skins.'

'I did.'

'And are you not—I remember you now—the very lad, the tanner's lad, that once pulled us ashore from the Eger—Cousin March and me?'

'Your memory is correct; I was that lad.'

'Thank'ee for it too. Lord! what a jolly life I should have missed! You got no reward, though. You threw away the guinea I offered you; come, I'll make it twenty guineas to-morrow.'

The insult was too much. 'Sir, you forget that whatever we may have been, to-night we meet as equals.'

'Equals!'

'As guests in the same house—most certainly, for the time being, equals.'

Richard Brithwood stared, literally dumb with fury. The standers-by were dumb too, though such *fracas* were then not uncommon even in drawing-rooms, and in women's presence, especially with men of Mr Brithwood's stamp. His wife seemed quite used to it. She merely shrugged her shoulders and hummed a note or two of '*Ça ira*'. It irritated the husband beyond all bounds.

'Hold your tongue, my lady. What, because a 'prentice lad once saved my life, and you choose to patronize him as you do many another vagabond, with your cursed liberty and equality, am I to have him at my table, and treat him as a gentleman? By——, madam, never!'

He spoke savagely and loud. John was silent; he had locked his hands together convulsively; but it was easy to see that his blood was at boiling heat, and that, did he once slip the leash of his passions, it would go hard with Richard Brithwood.

77

The latter came up to him with clenched fist. 'Now mark me, you—you vagabond!'

Ursula March crossed the room, and caught his arm, her eyes gleaming fire.

'Cousin, in my presence this gentleman shall be treated as a gentleman. He was kind to my father.'

'Curse your father!'

John's right hand burst free; he clutched the savage by the shoulder. 'Be silent. You had better.'

Brithwood shook off the grasp, turned and struck him; that last fatal insult, which offered from man to man, in those days, could only be wiped out with blood.

John staggered. For a moment he seemed as if he would have sprung on his adversary and felled him to the ground—but—he did not.

Some one whispered, 'He won't fight. He is a Quaker.'

'No!' he said, and stood erect; though he was ghastly pale, and his voice sounded hoarse and strange—'but I am a Christian; I shall not return blow for blow.'

In Central Africa

from *Bevis, The Story of a Boy* by Richard Jefferies

(Concerning the adventures of two highly imaginative boys . . .)

In front they could see nothing but the same endless reed-grass, except that there were more bushes and willows interspersed among it, showing that there must be numerous banks. Tired of holding on to the poles, which had no boughs of size enough to rest on, they let themselves gradually slide down. As they descended Mark spied a dove's nest in one of the hawthorn bushes; tired as he was he climbed up the pole again, and looked into it from a higher level. There was an egg in it; he had half a mind to take it, but remembered that it would be awkward to carry.

'We shall never get home,' he said, after he had told Bevis of the nest.

'Pooh,' said Bevis. 'Here's something for you to drink.' He had found a great teazle plant, whose leaves formed cups round the stem. In four of these cups there was a little darkish water, which had been there since the last shower. Mark eagerly sipped from the one which had the most, though it was full of drowned gnats; it moistened his lips, but he spluttered most of it out again. It was not only unpleasant to the taste, but warm.

'I hate Africa,' he shouted; 'I *hate* it.'

'So do I,' said Bevis; 'but we've got to get through it somehow.' He started again; Mark followed sullenly, and Pan came behind Mark. Thus the spaniel, stepping in the track they made, had the least difficulty of either. Pan's tail drooped, he was very hungry and very thirsty, and he knew it was about the time the dishes were rattling in the kitchen at home.

'Listen,' said Mark presently, putting his hand on Bevis's shoulder, and stopping him.

Bevis listened. 'I can't hear anything,' he said, 'except the midsummer hum.'

The hum was loud in the air above them, almost shrill, but there was not another sound. Now Mark had called attention to it, the noonday silence in that wild deserted place was strange.

'Where are all the things?' said Mark, looking round. 'All the birds have gone.'

Certainly they could hear none, even the brook-sparrows in the sedges by the New Sea were quiet. There was nothing in sight alive but a few swifts at an immense height above them. Neither woodpigeon, nor dove, nor thrush called; not even a yellow-hammer.

'I know,' whispered Bevis. 'I know—they are afraid.'

'Afraid?'

'Yes; can't you see Pan does not hunt about?'

'What is it?' asked Mark in an undertone, grasping his spear tightly. 'There are no mummies here?'

'No,' said Bevis. 'It's the serpent, you know; he's a hundred feet long; he's come over from the Unknown Island, and he's waiting in these sedges somewhere to catch something; the birds are afraid to sing.'

'Could he swallow a man?' said Mark.

'Swallow a man,' with curling lip. 'Swallow a buffalo easily.'

'Hush! what's that?' A puff of wind rustled the grasses.

'It's the snake!' said Mark, and off he tore, Bevis close behind him, Pan at his heels. In this wild panic they dashed quickly through the grasses, which just before had been so wearisome an obstacle. But the heat pulled them up in ten minutes, panting.

'Did you see him?' said Bevis.

'Just a little bit of him—I think,' said Mark.

'We've left him behind.'

'He'll find us by our track.'

'Let's tie Pan up, and let him swallow Pan.'

'Where's a rope? Have you any string? Give me your handkerchief.'

They were hastily tying their handkerchiefs together, when Mark, looking round to see if the monstrous serpent was approaching, shouted:

'There's a tree!'

There was a large hollow willow or pollard in the hedge. They rushed to it, they clasped it as shipwrecked men a beam. Mark was first, he got inside on the 'touchwood', and scrambled up a little way, then he worked up, his back against one side, and his knees the other. Bevis got underneath, and 'bunted' him up. Bunting is shoving with shoulder or hands. There were brambles on the top; Mark crushed through, and in a minute was firmly planted on the top.

'Give me my spear, and your bow, and your hand,' he said breathlessly.

The spear and bow were passed up: Bevis followed, taking Mark's hand just at the last. Mark put the point of his spear downwards to stab the monster. Bevis fitted an arrow to his bow. Pan looked up, but could not climb. They watched the long grasses narrowly, expecting to see them wave from side to side every instant, as the python wound his sinuous way. There was a rustling beneath, but on the other side of the hedge, Bevis looked and saw Pan, who had crept through.

'What are you going to do?' said Mark, as Bevis slung his bow on his shoulder as if it was a rifle, and began to move out on the hollow top of the tree, which as it became hollow had split, and partly arched over. Bevis did not answer: he crept cautiously out on the top, which vibrated under him; then suddenly seizing a lissom bough, he slipped off and let himself down.

The Interrogation

from *The Importance of Being Earnest* by Oscar Wilde

(John Worthing is kneeling to propose to Gwendolen Fairfax, when her mother, Lady Bracknell, enters the room)

Lady Bracknell   Mr Worthing! Rise, sir, from this semi-recumbent
posture. It is most indecorous.

Gwendolen   Mamma! (He tries to rise; she restrains him.) I must beg
you to retire. This is no place for you. Besides, Mr Worthing has
not quite finished yet.

Lady Bracknell   Finished what, may I ask?

Gwendolen   I am engaged to Mr Worthing, mamma. (They rise
together.)

Lady Bracknell   Pardon me, you are not engaged to any one. When
you do become engaged to some one, I, or your father, should his
health permit him, will inform you of the fact. An engagement
should come on a young girl as a surprise, pleasant or unpleasant, as the case may be. It is hardly a matter that she could
be allowed to arrange for herself. . . . And now I have a few
questions to put to you, Mr Worthing. While I am making these
inquiries, you, Gwendolen, will wait for me below in the carriage.

Gwendolen (reproachfully)   Mamma!

Lady Bracknell   In the carriage, Gwendolen! (*Gwendolen* goes to the
door. She and *Jack* blow kisses to each other behind *Lady Bracknell*'s back. *Lady Bracknell* looks vaguely about as if she could not
understand what the noise was. Finally turns round.) Gwendolen,
the carriage!

Gwendolen   Yes, mamma. (Goes out, looking back at *Jack*.)

Lady Bracknell (sitting down)   You can take a seat, Mr Worthing.
(Looks in her pocket for note-book and pencil.)

Jack   Thank you, Lady Bracknell, I prefer standing.

Lady Bracknell (pencil and note-book in hand)   I feel bound to tell
you that you are not down on my list of eligible young men,
although I have the same list as the dear Duchess of Bolton has.
We work together, in fact. However, I am quite ready to enter
your name, should your answers be what a really affectionate
mother requires. Do you smoke?

Jack   Well, yes, I must admit I smoke.

Lady Bracknell   I am glad to hear it. A man should always have an
occupation of some kind. There are far too many idle men in
London as it is. How old are you?

Jack   Twenty-nine.

Lady Bracknell   A very good age to be married at. I have always been of opinion that a man who desires to get married should know either everything or nothing. Which do you know?

Jack (after some hesitation) I know nothing, Lady Bracknell.

Lady Bracknell I am pleased to hear it. I do not approve of anything that tampers with natural ignorance. Ignorance is like a delicate exotic fruit; touch it and the bloom is gone. The whole theory of modern education is radically unsound. Fortunately in England, at any rate, education produces no effect whatsoever. If it did, it would prove a serious danger to the upper classes, and probably lead to acts of violence in Grosvenor Square. What is your income?

Jack Between seven and eight thousand a year.

Lady Bracknell (makes a note in her book) In land, or in investments?

Jack In investments, chiefly.

Lady Bracknell That is satisfactory. What between the duties expected of one during one's lifetime, and the duties exacted from one after one's death, land has ceased to be either a profit or a pleasure. It gives one position, and prevents one from keeping it up. That's all that can be said about land.

Jack I have a country house with some land, of course, attached to it, about fifteen hundred acres, I believe; but I don't depend on that for my real income. In fact, as far as I can make out, the poachers are the only people who make anything out of it.

Lady Bracknell A country house! How many bedrooms? Well, that point can be cleared up afterwards. You have a town house, I hope? A girl with a simple, unspoiled nature, like Gwendolen, could hardly be expected to reside in the country.

Jack Well, I own a house in Belgrave Square, but it is let by the year to Lady Bloxham. Of course, I can get it back whenever I like, at six months' notice.

Lady Bracknell Lady Bloxham? I don't know her.

Jack Oh, she goes about very little. She is a lady considerable advanced in years.

Lady Bracknell Ah, nowadays that is no guarantee of respectability of character. What number in Belgrave Square?

Jack 149.

Lady Bracknell (shaking her head) The unfashionable side. I thought there was something. However, that could easily be altered.

Jack Do you mean the fashion, or the side?

Lady Bracknell (sternly) Both, if necessary, I presume. What are your politics?

Jack Well, I am afraid I really have none. I am a Liberal Unionist.

Lady Bracknell Oh, they count as Tories. They dine with us. Or come in the evening, at any rate. Now to minor matters. Are your parents living?

Jack I have lost both my parents.

Lady Bracknell To lose one parent, Mr Worthing, may be regarded as a misfortune; to lose both looks like carelessness. Who was your father? He was evidently a man of some wealth. Was he born in what the Radical papers call the purple of commerce, or did he rise from the ranks of the aristocracy?

Jack I am afraid I really don't know. The fact is, Lady Bracknell, I said I had lost my parents. It would be nearer the truth to say that my parents seem to have lost me. . . . I don't actually know who I am by birth. I was . . . well, I was found.

Lady Bracknell Found!

Jack The late Mr Thomas Cardew, an old gentleman of a very charitable and kindly disposition, found me, and gave me the name of Worthing, because he happened to have a first-class ticket for Worthing in his pocket at the time. Worthing is a place in Sussex. It is a seaside resort.

Lady Bracknell Where did the charitable gentleman who had a first-class ticket for this seaside resort find you?

Jack (gravely) In a hand-bag.

Lady Bracknell A hand-bag?

Jack (very seriously) Yes, Lady Bracknell. I was in a hand-bag—a somewhat large, black leather hand-bag, with handles to it—an ordinary hand-bag, in fact.

Lady Bracknell In what locality did this Mr James, or Thomas, Cardew come across this ordinary hand-bag?

Jack In the cloak-room at Victoria Station. It was given to him in mistake for his own.

Lady Bracknell The cloak-room at Victoria Station?

Jack Yes, the Brighton line.

Lady Bracknell The line is immaterial. Mr Worthing, I confess I feel somewhat bewildered by what you have just told me. To be born, or at any rate bred, in a hand-bag, whether it had handles or not, seems to me to display a contempt for the ordinary decencies of family life that reminds one of the worst excesses of the French Revolution. And I presume you know what that unfortunate movement led to? As for the particular locality in which the hand-bag was found, a cloak-room at a railway station might serve to conceal a social indiscretion—has probably, indeed, been used for that purpose before now—but it could hardly be regarded as an assured basis for a recognised position in good society.

Jack May I ask you then what you would advise me to do? I need hardly say I would do anything in the world to ensure Gwendolen's happiness.

Lady Bracknell I would strongly advise you, Mr Worthing, to try and acquire some relations as soon as possible, and to make a definite effort to produce at any rate one parent, of either sex, before the season is quite over.

Jack Well, I don't see how I could possibly manage to do that. I can produce the hand-bag, at any moment. It is in my dressing-room at home. I really think that should satisfy you, Lady Bracknell.

Lady Bracknell Me, sir! What has it to do with me? You can hardly imagine that I and Lord Bracknell would dream of allowing our only daughter—a girl brought up with the utmost care—to marry into a cloak-room, and form an alliance with a parcel. Goodmorning, Mr Worthing!

(*Lady Bracknell* sweeps out in majestic indignation.)

Daniel O'Rourke tells his Story

from *Daniel O'Rourke* by Thomas Crofton Croker

To make a long story short, I got, as a body may say, the same thing as tipsy almost, for I can't remember ever at all, no ways, how it was I left the place: only I did leave it, that's certain. Well, I thought, for all that, in myself, I'd just step to Molly Cronohan's, the fairy-woman, to speak a word about the bracket heifer that was bewitched; and so as I was crossing the stepping-stones of the ford of Ballyasheenough, and was looking up at the stars, and blessing myself—for why? it was Lady-day—I missed my foot, and souse I fell into the water. 'Death alive!' thought I, 'I'll be drowned now!'

However, I began swimming, swimming, swimming away for the dear life, till at last I got ashore, somehow or other, but never the one of me can tell how, upon a *dissolute* island.

I wandered and wandered about there, without knowing where I wandered, until at last I got into a big bog. The moon was shining as bright as day, or your fair lady's eyes, sir (with your pardon for mentioning her) and I looked east and west, and north and south, and every way, and nothing did I see but bog, bog, bog;—I could never find out how I got into it; and my heart grew cold with fear, for sure and certain I was that it would be my *berrin* place. So I sat down upon a stone, which, as good luck would have it, was close by me; and I began to scratch my head and sing the *Ullagone*—when all of a sudden the moon grew black, and I looked up, and saw something for all the world as if it was moving down between me and it, and I could not tell what it was. Down it came with a pounce, and looked at me full in the face; and what was it but an eagle? as fine as one as ever flew from the kingdom of Kerry.

So he looked at me in the face, and says he to me, 'Daniel O'Rourke,' says he, 'how do you do?'

'Very well, I thank you, sir,' says I; 'I hope you're well'; wondering out of my senses all the time how an eagle came to speak like a Christian.

'What brings you here, Dan?' says he.

'Nothing at all, sir,' says I; 'only I wish I was safe home again.'

'Is it out of the island you want to go, Dan?' says he.

''Tis, sir,' says I; so I up and told him how I had taken a drop too much; and fell into the water; how I swam to the island; and how I got into the bog and did not know my way out of it.

'Dan,' says he after a minute's thought, 'though it is very improper for you to get drunk on Lady-day, yet as you are a decent sober man, who 'tends mass well, and never flings stones at me nor mine, nor cries out after us in the fields—my life for yours,' says he; 'so get up on my back, and grip me well for fear you'd fall off, and I'll fly you out of the bog.'

'I am afraid,' says I, 'your honour's making game of me; for who ever heard of riding a-horseback on an eagle before?'

''Pon the honour of a gentleman,' says he, putting his right foot on his breast, 'I am quite in earnest; and so now either take my offer or starve in the bog; besides, I see that your weight is sinking the stone.'

It was true enough as he said, for I found the stone every minute going from under me. I had no choice; so thinks I to myself, faint heart never won fair lady, and this is fair persuadance—'I thank your honour,' says I, 'for the loan of your civility, and I'll take your kind offer.'

I therefore mounted upon the back of the eagle, and held him tight enough by the throat, and up he flew in the air, like a lark. Little I knew the trick he was going to serve up. Up, up up—God knows how far up he flew.

'Why, then,' said I to him—thinking he did not know the right road home—very civilly, because why?—I was in his power entirely; —'sir,' says I, 'please your honour's glory, and with humble submission to your better judgment, if you'd fly down a bit, you're now just over my cabin, and I could be put down there, and many thanks to your worship.'

'*Arrah*, Dan,' said he, 'do you think me a fool? Look down in the next field, and don't you see two men and a gun? By my word it would be no joke to be shot this way, to oblige a drunken blackguard that I picked up off a *could* stone in a bog.'

'Bother you,' said I to myself, but I did not speak out, for where was the use? Well, sir, up he kept flying, flying, and I asking him every minute to fly down, and all to no use.

'Where in the world are you going, sir?' says I to him.

'Hold your tongue, Dan,' says he; 'mind your own business, and don't be interfering with the business of other people.'

'Faith, this is my business, I think,' says I.

'Be quiet, Dan,' says he; so I said no more.

'At last where should we come but to the moon itself. Now you can't see it from this, but there is, or there was in my time, a reaping-hook sticking out of the side of the moon, this way (drawing the figure on the ground with the end of his stick).

'Dan,' said the eagle, 'I'm tired with this long fly; I had no notion 'twas so far.'

'And my lord, sir,' said I, 'who in the world *axed* you to fly so far—was it I? Did not I beg, and pray, and beseech you to stop half an hour ago?'

'There's no use talking, Dan,' said he; 'I'm tired bad enough, so you must get off and sit down on the moon until I rest myself.'

'Is it sit down on the moon?' said I; 'is it upon that little round thing, then? why then, sure, I'd fall off in a minute, and be *kilt* and split, and smashed all to bits: you are a vile deceiver—so you are.'

'Not at all, Dan,' said he; 'you can catch fast hold of the reaping-hook that's sticking out of the side of the moon, and 'twill keep you up.'

'I won't then,' said I.

'Maybe not,' said he quite quiet. 'If you don't, my man, I shall just give you a shake, and one slap of my wing, and send you down to the ground, where every bone in your body will be smashed as small as a drop of dew on a cabbage-leaf in the morning.'

'Why, then, I'm in a fine way,' said I to myself, 'ever to have come along with the likes of you'; and so giving him a hearty curse in Irish, for fear he'd know what I said, I got off his back with a heavy heart, took a hold of the reaping-hook, and sat down upon the moon; and a mighty cold seat it was, I can tell you that.

When he had me there fairly landed, he turned about on me, and said, 'Good-morning to you, Daniel O'Rourke,' said he, 'I think I've nicked you fairly now. You robbed my nest last year' ('twas true enough for him, but how he found it out is hard to say), 'and in return you are freely welcome to cool your heels dangling upon the moon like a cockthrow.'

'Is that all, and is this the way you leave me, you brute you!' says I. 'You ugly unnatural *baste*, and is this the way you serve me at last? Bad luck to yourself, with your hook'd nose, and to all your breed, you blackguard.'

'Twas all to no manner of use; he spread out his great big wings, burst out a-laughing, and flew away like lightning. I bawled after him to stop; but I might have called and bawled for ever without his minding me. Away he went, and I never saw him from that day to this—sorrow fly away with him! You may be sure I was in a disconsolate condition, and kept roaring out for the bare grief, when all at once a door opened right in the middle of the moon, creaking on its hinges as if it had not been opened for a month before—I suppose they never thought of greasing 'em,—and out there walks—who do you think but the man in the moon himself? I knew him by his bush.

'Good-morrow to you, Daniel O'Rourke,' said he: 'how do you do?'

'Very well, thank your honour,' said I. 'I hope your honour's well.'

The Mock Turtle's Story

from *Alice in Wonderland* by Lewis Carroll

They had not gone far before they saw the Mock Turtle in the distance, sitting sad and lonely on a little ledge of rock, and, as they came nearer, Alice could hear him sighing as if his heart would break.

She pitied him deeply. 'What is his sorrow?' she asked the Gryphon, and the Gryphon answered, very nearly in the same words as before: 'It's all his fancy, that: he hasn't got no sorrow, you know. Come on!'

So they went up to the Mock Turtle, who looked at them with large eyes full of tears, but said nothing.

'This here young lady,' said the Gryphon, 'she wants for to know your history, she do.'

'I'll tell it her,' said the Mock Turtle in a deep, hollow tone: 'sit down, both of you, and don't speak a word till I've finished.'

So they sat down, and nobody spoke for some minutes. Alice thought to herself: 'I don't see how he can *ever* finish, if he doesn't begin.' But she waited patiently.

'Once,' said the Mock Turtle at last, with a deep sigh, 'I was a real Turtle.'

These words were followed by a very long silence, broken only by an occasional exclamation of 'Hjckrrh!' from the Gryphon, and the constant heavy sobbing of the Mock Turtle. Alice was very nearly getting up and saying: 'Thank you, sir, for your interesting story,' but she could not help thinking there *must* be more to come, so she sat still and said nothing.

'When we were little,' the Mock Turtle went on at last, more calmly, though still sobbing a little now and then, 'we went to school in the sea. The master was an old Turtle—we used to call him Tortoise——'

'Why did you call him Tortoise, if he wasn't one?' Alice asked.

'We called him Tortoise because he taught us,' said the Mock Turtle angrily: 'really you are very dull!'

'You ought to be ashamed of yourself for asking such a simple question,' added the Gryphon; and then they both sat silent and looked at poor Alice, who felt ready to sink into the earth. At last the Gryphon said to the Mock Turtle: 'Drive on, old fellow! Don't be all day about it!' and he went on in these words:

'Yes, we went to school in the sea, though you mayn't believe it——'

'I never said I didn't!' interrupted Alice.

'You did,' said the Mock Turtle.

'Hold your tongue!' added the Gryphon, before Alice could speak again. The Mock Turtle went on:

'We had the best of educations—in fact, we went to school every day——'

'*I've* been to a day-school too,' said Alice; 'you needn't be so proud as all that.'

'With extras?' asked the Mock Turtle a little anxiously.

'Yes,' said Alice, 'we learned French and music.'

'And washing?' said the Mock Turtle.

'Certainly not!' said Alice indignantly.

'Ah! then yours wasn't a really good school,' said the Mock Turtle in a tone of great relief. 'Now at *ours* they had at the end of the bill: "French, music, *and washing*—extra."'

'You couldn't have wanted it much,' said Alice; 'living at the bottom of the sea.'

'I couldn't afford to learn it,' said the Mock Turtle with a sigh. 'I only took the regular course.'

'What was that?' inquired Alice.

'Reeling and Writhing, of course, to begin with,' the Mock Turtle replied; 'and then the different branches of Arithmetic—Ambition, Distraction, Uglification and Derision.'

'I never heard of "Uglification,"' Alice ventured to say. 'What is it?'

The Gryphon lifted up both its paws in surprise. 'What! Never heard of uglifying!' it exclaimed. 'You know what to beautify is, I suppose?'

'Yes,' said Alice doubtfully: 'it means—to—make—anything—prettier.'

'Well, then,' the Gryphon went on, 'if you don't know what to uglify is, you *must* be a simpleton.'

Alice did not feel encouraged to ask any more questions about it, so she turned to the Mock Turtle, and said: 'What else had you to learn?'

'Well, there was Mystery,' the Mock Turtle replied, counting off the subjects on his flappers, '——Mystery ancient and modern, with Seaography: then Drawling—the Drawling-master was an old conger-eel, that used to come once a week: *he* taught us Drawling, Stretching, and Fainting in Coils.'

'What was *that* like?' said Alice.

'Well, I can't show it you myself,' the Mock Turtle said: 'I'm too stiff. And the Gryphon never learnt it.'

'Hadn't time,' said the Gryphon: 'I went to the Classical master, though. He was an old crab, *he* was.'

'I never went to him,' the Mock Turtle said with a sigh: 'he taught Laughing and Grief, they used to say.'

'So he did, so he did,' said the Gryphon, sighing in his turn; and both creatures hid their faces in their paws.

'And how many hours a day did you do lessons?' said Alice, in a hurry to change the subject.

'Ten hours the first day,' said the Mock Turtle: 'nine the next, and so on.'

'What a curious plan!' exclaimed Alice.

'That's the reason they're called lessons,' the Gryphon remarked: 'because they lessen from day to day.'

This was quite a new idea to Alice, and she thought it over a little before she made her next remark. 'Then the eleventh day must have been a holiday?'

'Of course it was,' said the Mock Turtle.

'And how did you manage on the twelfth?' Alice went on eagerly.

'That's enough of lessons,' the Gryphon interrupted in a very decided tone: 'tell her something about the games now.'

The Cop and the Anthem

a short story by O. Henry (abridged)

On his bench in Madison Square Soapy moved uneasily. When wild goose honk high of nights, and when women without sealskin coats grow kind to their husbands, and when Soapy moves uneasily on his bench in the park, you may know that winter is near at hand.

The hibernatorial ambitions of Soapy were not of the highest. In them were no considerations of Mediterranean cruises, of soporific Southern skies or drifting in the Vesuvian Bay. Three months on the Island was what his soul craved. Three months of assured board and bed and congenial company, safe from Boreas and bluecoats, seemed to Soapy the essence of things desirable.

For years the hospitable Blackwell's had been his winter quarters. Just as his more fortunate fellow New Yorkers had bought their tickets to Palm Beach and the Riviera each winter, so Soapy had made his humble arrangements for his annual hegira to the Island. And now the time was come. On the previous night three Sabbath newspapers, distributed beneath his coat, about his ankles and over his lap, had failed to repulse the cold as he slept on his bench near the spurting fountain in the ancient square. So the Island loomed large and timely in Soapy's mind. He scorned the provisions made in the name of charity for the city's dependants. In Soapy's opinion the Law was more benign than Philanthropy. There was an endless round of institutions, municipal and eleemosynary, on which he might set out and receive lodging and food accordant with the simple life. But to one of Soapy's proud spirit the gifts of charity are encumbered. If not in coin you must pay in humiliation of spirit for every benefit received at the hands of philanthropy. As Caesar had his Brutus, every bed of charity must have its toll of a bath, every loaf of bread its compensation of a private and personal inquisition. Wherefore it is better to be a guest of the law, which though conducted by rules, does not meddle unduly with a gentleman's private affairs.

Soapy, having decided to go to the Island, at once set about accomplishing his desire. There were many easy ways of doing this. The pleasantest was to dine luxuriously at some expensive restaurant; and then, after declaring insolvency, be handed over quietly and without uproar to a policeman. An accommodating magistrate would do the rest.

Soapy left his bench and strolled out of the square and across the level sea of asphalt, where Broadway and Fifth Avenue flow together. Up Broadway he turned, and halted at a glittering café, where are gathered together nightly the choicest products of the grape, the silk-worm and the protoplasm.

Soapy had confidence in himself from the lowest button of his vest upward. He was shaven, and his coat was decent and his neat black, ready-tied four-in-hand had been presented to him by a lady missionary on Thanksgiving Day. If he could reach a table in the restaurant unsuspected, success would be his. The portion of him that would show above the table would raise no doubt in the waiter's mind. A roasted mallard duck, thought Soapy, would be about the thing—with a bottle of Chablis, and the Camembert, a demi-tasse and a cigar. One dollar for the cigar would be enough. The total would not be so high as to call forth any supreme manifestation of revenge from the café management; and yet the meat would leave him filled and happy for the journey to his winter refuge.

But as Soapy set foot inside the restaurant door the head waiter's eye fell upon his frayed trousers and decadent shoes. Strong and ready hands turned him about and conveyed him in silence and haste to the sidewalk and averted the ignoble fate of the menaced mallard.

Soapy turned off Broadway. It seemed that his route to the coveted island was not to be an epicurean one. Some other way of entering limbo must be thought of.

91

At a corner of Sixth Avenue electric lights and cunningly displayed wares behind plate-glass made a shop window conspicuous. Soapy took a cobble-stone and dashed it through the glass. People came running round the corner, a policeman in the lead. Soapy stood still, with his hands in his pockets, and smiled at the sight of brass buttons.

'Where's the man that done that?' inquired the officer excitedly.

'Don't you figure out that I might have had something to do with it?' said Soapy, not without sarcasm, but friendly, as one greets good fortune.

The policeman's mind refused to accept Soapy even as a clue. Men who smash windows do not remain to parley with the law's minions. They take to their heels. The policeman saw a man halfway down the block running to catch a car. With drawn club he joined in the pursuit. Soapy, with disgust in his heart, loafed along, twice unsuccessful.

On the opposite side of the street was a restaurant of no great pretensions. It catered to large appetites and modest purses. Its crockery and atmosphere were thick; its soup and napery thin. Into this place Soapy took his accusive shoes and tell-tale trousers without challenge. At a table he sat and consumed beefsteak, flapjacks, doughnuts, and pie. And then to the waiter he betrayed the fact that the minutest coin and himself were strangers.

'Now, get busy and call a cop,' said Soapy. 'And don't keep a gentleman waiting.'

'No cop for youse,' said the waiter, with a voice like butter cakes and an eye like the cherry in a Manhattan cocktail. 'Hey, Con!'

Neatly upon his left ear on the callous pavement two waiters pitched Soapy. He arose, joint by joint, as a carpenter's rule opens, and beat the dust from his clothes. Arrest seemed but a rosy dream. The Island seemed very far away. A policeman who stood before a drug store two doors away laughed and walked down the street.

A sudden fear seized Soapy that some dreadful enchantment had rendered him immune to arrest. The thought brought a little of panic upon it, and when he came upon another policeman lounging grandly in front of a transplendent theatre he caught at the immediate straw of 'disorderly conduct'.

On the sidewalk Soapy began to yell drunken gibberish at the top of his harsh voice. He danced, howled, raved, and otherwise disturbed the welkin.

The policeman twirled his club, turned his back to Soapy and remarked to a citizen:

''Tis one of them Yale lads celebratin' the goose egg they give to the Hartford College. Noisy; but no harm. We've instructions to lave them be.'

Disconsolate, Soapy ceased his unavailing racket. Would never a policeman lay hands on him? In his fancy the Island seemed an unattainable Arcadia. He buttoned his thin coat against the chilling wind.

In a cigar store he saw a well-dressed man lighting a cigar at a swinging light. His silk umbrella he had set by the door on entering. Soapy stepped inside, secured the umbrella and sauntered off with it slowly. The man at the cigar light followed hastily.

'My umbrella,' he said sternly.

'Oh, is it?' sneered Soapy, adding insult to petit larceny. 'Well, why don't you call a policeman? I took it. Your umbrella! Why don't you call a cop? There stands one on the corner.'

The umbrella owner slowed his steps. Soapy did likewise, with a presentiment that luck would run against him. The policeman looked at the two curiously.

'Of course,' said the umbrella man—'that is—well, you know how these mistakes occur—I—if it's your umbrella I hope you'll excuse me—I picked it up this morning in a restaurant—if you recognise it as yours, why—I hope you'll——'

'Of course it's mine,' said Soapy viciously.

The ex-umbrella man retreated. The policeman hurried to assist a tall blonde in an opera cloak across the street in front of a street car that was approaching two blocks away.

Soapy walked eastward through a street damaged by improvements. He hurled the umbrella wrathfully into an excavation. He muttered against the men who wear helmets and carry clubs. Because he wanted to fall into their clutches, they seemed to regard him as a king who could do no wrong.

At length Soapy reached one of the avenues to the east where the glitter and turmoil was but faint. He set his face down this toward Madison Square, for the homing instinct survives even when the home is a park bench.

But on an unusually quiet corner Soapy came to a standstill. Here was an old church, quaint and rambling and gabled. Through one violet-stained window a soft light glowed, where, no doubt, the organist loitered over the keys, making sure of his mastery of the coming Sabbath anthem. For there drifted out to Soapy's ears sweet music that caught and held him transfixed against the convolutions of the iron fence.

The moon was above, lustrous and serene; vehicles and pedestrians were few; sparrows twittered sleepily in the eaves—for a little while the scene might have been a country churchyard. And the anthem that the organist played cemented Soapy to the iron fence, for he had known it well in the days when his life contained such things as mothers and roses and ambitions and friends and immaculate thoughts and collars.

The conjunction of Soapy's receptive state of mind and the influences about the old church wrought a sudden and wonderful change in his soul. He viewed with swift horror the pit into which he had tumbled, the degraded days, unworthy desires, dead hopes, wrecked faculties, and base motives that made up his existence.

And also in a moment his heart responded thrillingly to this novel mood. An instantaneous and strong impulse moved him to battle with his desperate fate. He would pull himself out of the mire; he would make a man of himself again; he would conquer the evil that had taken possession of him. There was time; he was comparatively young yet; he would resurrect his old eager ambitions and pursue them without faltering. Those solemn but sweet organ notes had set up a revolution in him. To-morrow he would go into the roaring downtown district and find work. A fur importer had once offered him a place as driver. He would find him to-morrow and ask for the position. He would be somebody in the world.

He would——

Soapy felt a hand laid on his arm. He looked quickly round into the broad face of a policeman.

'What are you doin' here?' asked the officer.

'Nothin',' said Soapy.

'Then come along,' said the policeman.

'Three months on the Island,' said the Magistrate in the Police Court the next morning.

The Letter

from *Handy Andy* by Samuel Lover

(This portrait of Irish life in the nineteenth century is introduced by the author as follows: 'Andy Rooney was a fellow who had the most singular ingenious knack of doing everything the wrong way; disappointment waited on all affairs in which he bore a part, and destruction was at his finger's ends: so the nickname the neighbours stuck upon him was Handy Andy . . .')

'Ride into the town, and see if there's a letter for me,' said the squire one day to our hero.

'Yis, sir.'

'You know where to go?'

'To the town, sir.'

'But do you know where to go in the town?'

'No, sir.'

'And why don't you ask, you stupid thief?'

'Sure, I'd find out, sir.'

'Didn't I often tell you to ask what you're to do when you don't know?'

'Yis, sir.'

'And why don't you?'

'I don't like to be troublesome, sir.'

'Confound you. Well, go to the post-office. You know the post-office, I suppose?'

'Yes, sir. Where they sell gun-powder.'

'You're right for once,' said the squire; for his Majesty's postmaster was the person who had the privilege of dealing in the aforesaid combustible. 'Go then to the post-office and ask for a letter for me. Remember—not gun-powder, but a letter.'

'Yes, sir,' said Andy, who got astride of his hack and trotted away to the post-office. On arriving at the shop of the postmaster (for that person carried on a brisk trade in groceries, gimlets, broad-cloth and linen-drapery) Andy presented himself at the counter, and said:

'I want a letther, sir, if you plaze.'

'Who do you want it for?' said the postmaster, in a tone which Andy considered an aggression upon the sacredness of private life: so Andy thought the coolest contempt he could throw upon the prying impertinence of the postmaster was to repeat his question.

'I want a letther, sir, if you plaze.'

'And who do you want it for?' repeated the postmaster.

'What's that to you?' said Andy.

The postmaster, laughing at his simplicity, told him he could not tell what letter to give him unless he told him the direction.

'The directions I got was to get a letther here—that's the directions.'

'Who gave you these directions?'

'The master.'

'And who's your master?'

'What consarn is that o' yours?'

'Why, you stupid rascal, if you don't tell me his name, how can I give you a letter?'

'You could give it, if you liked; but you're fond of axin' impident questions, bekaze you think I'm simple.'

'Go along out o' this. Your master must be as great a goose as yourself to send such a messenger.'

'Bad luck to your impidence,' said Andy; 'is it Squire Egan you dare to say goose to?'

'Oh, Squire Egan's your master then?'

'Yis. Have you anything to say agin it?'

'Only that I never saw you before.'

'Faith, then you'll never see me again if I have my own consint.'

'I won't give you any letter for the squire, unless I know you're his servant. Is there any one in the town knows you?'

'Plenty,' said Andy, 'it's not every one is as ignorant as you.'

Just at this moment a person to whom Andy was known entered the house, who vouchsafed to the postmaster that he might give Andy the squire's letter. 'Have you one for me?'

'Yes, sir,' said the postmaster, producing one—'fourpence.'

The gentleman paid the fourpence postage, and left the shop with his letter.

'Here's a letter for the squire,' said the postmaster, 'you've to pay me elevenpence postage.'

'What 'ud I pay elevenpence for?'

'For postage.'

'To the devil wid you. Didn't I see you give Mr Durthy a letther for fourpence this minit, and a bigger letther than this? And now you want me to pay elevenpence for this scrap of a thing. Do you think I'm a fool?'

'No, but I'm sure of it,' said the postmaster.

'Well, you're welkim to be sure, sure;—but don't be delayin' me now; here's fourpence for you, and gi' me the letther.'

'Go along you stupid thief,' said the postmaster, taking up the letter, and going to serve a customer with a mousetrap.

While this person and many others were served, Andy lounged up and down the shop, every now and then putting in his head in the middle of the customers, and saying, 'Will you gi' me the letther?'

He waited for above half an hour, in defiance of the anathemas of the postmaster, and at last left, when he found it impossible to get common justice for his master, which he thought he deserved as well as another man; for, under this impression, Andy determined to give no more than the fourpence.

The squire in the meantime was getting impatient for his return and when Andy made his appearance asked if there was a letter for him.

'There is, sir,' said Andy.

'Then give it to me.'

'I haven't it, sir.'

'What do you mean?'

'He wouldn't give it to me, sir.'

'Who wouldn't give it to you?'

'That owld chate beyant in the town,—wanting to charge double for it.'

'Maybe it's a double letter. Why the devil didn't you pay what he asked, sir?'

'Arrah, sir, why should I let you be chated? It's not a double letther at all: not above half the size o' one Mr Durthy got before my face for fourpence.'

'You'll provoke me to break your neck some day, you vagabond. Ride back for your life, you omadhaun, and pay whatever he asks and get me the letter.'

'Why, sir, I tell you he was sellin' them before my face for fourpence a-piece.'

'Go back you scoundrel, or I'll horsewhip you; and if you're longer than an hour, I'll have you ducked in the horsepond.'

Andy vanished and made a second visit to the post-office. When he arrived two other persons were getting letters and the postmaster was selecting the epistles for each, from a large parcel that lay before him on the counter; and at the same time many shop customers were waiting to be served.

'I'm come for that letther,' said Andy.

'I'll attend to you by-and-by.'

'The masther's in a hurry.'

'Let him wait till his hurry's over.'

97

'He'll murther me if I'm not back soon.'

'I'm glad to hear it.'

While the postmaster went on with such provoking answers to these appeals for despatch, Andy's eye caught the heap of letters which lay on the counter; so while certain weighing of soap and tobacco was going forward, he contrived to become possessed of two letters from the heap, and having effected that, waited patiently enough till it was the great man's pleasure to give him the missive directed to his master.

Then did Andy bestride his hack, and in triumph at his trick on the postmaster, rattle along the road homeward as fast as the beast could carry him. He came into the squire's presence, his face beaming with delight, and an air of self-satisfied superiority in his manner, quite unaccountable to his master, until he pulled forth his hand, which had been grubbing up his prizes from the bottom of his pocket; and holding three letters over his head, while he said, 'Look at that!' he next slapped them down under his broad fist on the table before the squire, saying:

'Well! if he did make me pay elevenpence, by gor, I brought your honour the worth o' your money any how!'

The Duel

from *Christie Johnstone* by Charles Reade

He met Lord Ipsden, and said at once, in his wise temperate way: 'Sir, you are a villain!'

Ipsden   *Plaît-il?*

Gatty   You are a villain!

Ipsden   How do you make that out?

Gatty   But, of course, you are not a coward, too.

Ipsden (ironically)   You surprise me with your moderation, Sir.

Gatty   Then you will waive your rank,—you are a Lord, I believe,—and give me satisfaction.

Ipsden   My rank, Sir, such as it is, engages me to give a proper answer to proposals of this sort; I am at your orders.

Gatty   A man of your character must often have been called to an account by your victims, so—so—(hesitating)—perhaps you will tell me the proper course.

Ipsden   *I* shall send a note to the castle, and the Colonel will send me down somebody with a moustache; I shall pretend to remember moustache, moustache will pretend he remembers me; he will then communicate with your friend, and they will arrange it all for us.

Gatty And, perhaps, through your licentiousness, one or both of us will be killed.

Ipsden Yes! but we need not trouble our heads about that,—the seconds undertake everything.

Gatty I have no pistols.

Ipsden If you will do me the honour to use one of mine, it shall be at your service.

Gatty Thank you.

Ipsden To-morrow morning.

Gatty No. I have four days' painting to do on my picture, I can't die till it is finished;—Friday morning.

Ipsden (He is mad) I wish to ask you a question, you will excuse my curiosity. Have you any idea what we are agreeing to differ about?

Gatty The question does you little credit, my Lord; that is to add insult to wrong.

He went off hurriedly, leaving Lord Ipsden mystified.

On Friday morning, then, there paced on Leith Sands two figures.

One was Lord Ipsden.

Gatty came up.

They saluted.

'Where is your second, Sir?' said the Maréchal.

'My second?' said Gatty. 'Ah! I forgot to wake him—does it matter?'

'It is merely a custom,' said Lord Ipsden, with a very slightly satirical manner. 'Savanadero,' said he, 'do us the honour to measure the ground, and be everybody's second.'

Savanadero measured the ground, and handed a pistol to each combatant, and struck an imposing attitude apart.

'Are you ready, gentlemen?' said this Jack-o'-both-sides.

'Yes!' said both.

Just as the signal was about to be given, an interruption occurred. 'I beg your pardon, Sir,' said Lord Ipsden to his antagonist; 'I am going to take a *liberty—a great liberty* with you, but I think you will find your pistol is only at half-cock.'

'Thank you, my Lord; what am I to do with the thing?'

99

'Draw back the cock so, and be ready to fire.'

'So?' *Bang!*

He had touched the trigger as well as the cock, so off went the barker; and after a considerable pause the Field-Marshal sprang yelling into the air.

'Hallo!' cried Mr Gatty.

'Ah! oh! I'm a dead man,' whined the General.

'Nonsense!' said Ipsden, after a moment of anxiety. 'Give yourself no concern, Sir,' said he, soothingly, to his antagonist—'A mere accident.—Maréchal, reload Mr Gatty's pistol.'

'Excuse me, my Lord——'

'Load his pistol directly,' said his Lordship sternly; 'and behave like a gentleman.'

'My Lord! my Lord! but where shall I stand to be safe?'

'Behind me!'

The Commander of Division advanced reluctantly for Gatty's pistol.

'No, my Lord!' said Gatty, 'it is plain I am not a fit antagonist; I shall but expose myself—and my mother has separated us; I have lost her—if you do not win her, some worse man may; but oh if you are a man use her tenderly.'

'Whom?'

'Christie Johnstone! Oh, Sir, do not make her regret me too much! She was my treasure, my consolation,—she was to be my wife, she would have cheered the road of life—it is a desert now. I loved her—I—I——'

Here the poor fellow choked.

Lord Ipsden turned round, and threw his pistol to Saunders, saying, 'Catch that, Saunders.'

Saunders, on the contrary, by a single motion changed his person from a vertical straight line to a horizontal line, exactly parallel with the earth's surface, and the weapon sang innoxious over him.

His Lordship then, with a noble defiance of etiquette, walked up to his antagonist and gave him his hand, with a motion no one could resist;—for he felt for the poor fellow.

'It is all a mistake,' said he. 'There is no sentiment between La Johnstone and me but mutual esteem. I will explain the whole thing; *I* admire *her* for her virtue, her wit, her innocence, her goodness, and all that sort of thing; and *she*—what *she* sees in *me*, I am sure I don't know,' added he, slightly shrugging his aristocratic shoulders. 'Do me the honour to breakfast with me at Newhaven.'

III

Improvisations based on detailed instructions to each character

III Improvisations based on detailed instructions to each character

Introductory note

Each actor in the improvisation is given a detailed set of instructions which he follows closely, but each actor is unaware of the instructions given to the others. The instructions must be given individually, no one else being present except those who are not actually in the scene. This kind of improvisation calls for a slightly different type of imagination and concentration. Once a group has become familiar with the idiom they can start writing their own instruction sheets. Each character should have the instructions read to him twice, or should himself read them through a couple of times, so that he becomes really sure of the details.

Suspicion

Characters:
> Mrs Brownlow
> Wally, her son
> Mrs Manning, her neighbour
> Peter Goodman, her lodger

Instructions for THE LANDLADY
Your name is Mrs Brownlow. You are a widow and for the past ten years or so you have added to your small pension by taking a lodger for whom you provide a room and breakfast for the sum of five guineas a week. You have two children—Jack, who has now grown up and emigrated to Australia, and Wally, who is thirteen years old and still at school. You are very fond of Wally, but he's seldom at home, since he spends all his free time out cycling with his mates. All that Wally ever seems to want from you is his pocket money, and even then he usually complains that you don't give him enough. You don't have many friends, and you don't really approve of being too friendly with the neighbours. But Mrs Manning who lives next door keeps on calling in for the occasional cup of tea or to borrow some sugar or perhaps some baking powder, and you have become very annoyed about this. And Mrs Manning never seems to return or pay for any

of the goods that she 'borrows'. As a consequence of this, the last time she knocked on your door you at first pretended to be out, and when Mrs Manning kept on knocking you eventually opened the door and told her off for troubling you so often and for being generally something of a nuisance. Mrs Manning was about to answer you when you shut the door and that was that.

You have recently taken a new lodger, and since you only have room for one lodger at a time this is quite an important event in your life. The last lodger was not very pleasant—you didn't really like the look of him and you were not too sure that he was completely respectable, so you asked him to find lodgings elsewhere. The new lodger is a young man of about twenty-five and he works at the local branch of the Electricity Board. All went well until this morning, when the lodger, whose name is Mr Goodman, went off to work leaving his wallet on the table. As a favour to him you walked down the road to the telephone box at the corner, phoned up the Electricity Board and asked to speak to him. Your intention was to tell him that he had left his wallet at home and there was no need for him to worry whether he had lost it. To your surprise you found that there was no such person as Mr Goodman working at the Electricity Board and never had been. You became rather suspicious, and then you remembered that a few weeks ago there were photographs in the newspaper of a dangerous criminal who was on the loose and who was reported to have been seen in your area. He was wanted by the police for questioning in connection with a number of major robberies. And now that you think about it, there is a striking resemblance between Mr Goodman and the wanted man. But you are a very cool and capable person, so you don't panic. It's only one o'clock. Mr Goodman never gets back until seven in the evening, and Wally will be home for lunch any minute now, so you can chat with him about it. Or you might even call on Mrs Manning and have a chat with her about it. But that might be rather embarrassing. After all, you were rather brisk with Mrs Manning the last time she called on you. But then, this is important. You might even take a stroll round to the police station, when the fog clears, and at the moment the fog is getting rather worse.

AT THE MOMENT you are preparing lunch for yourself and Wally.

Instructions for THE SON
Your name is Wally Brownlow. You are thirteen years old and you

are attending a local secondary school. You live with your mother in a semi-detached house in a London suburb, and your father died when you were very young. You're quite fond of your mother in your own way, and you're really very keen to do anything you can to help her, but she always wants you to stay indoors, when you, quite rightly, always want to get out of doors and join your mates. Your great hobby is cycling, and this takes up all your spare time. When you grow up you want to be a champion cyclist and enter international contests. At the moment you are saving up to buy a special sports cycle which is rather expensive and which you will not be able to afford for another few months yet. Well, it looked like this, until this morning when one of your friends at school told you that his brother is selling the very cycle that you want, only slightly used, for six pounds—this is a lot cheaper than a new model, and it is only two pounds more than what you have saved up already. But the money must be found today, or the bike will be sold to someone else. You decide to ask your mother when you see her at lunch-time, but you're not too optimistic about the possible success of this. Your mother is never very generous with her money, and you also know that she does not have very much to be generous with. But you will see what you can do. You never know. She may be in a good mood. And you can always try to bribe her into giving or lending you the money by offering to work extra hard at your school work, or by offering to spend more time at home.

If you are unable to get the money from your mother, then you will wait until the evening and have a word with the lodger, Mr Goodman. He's very pleasant, and a few weeks ago, he gave you ten shillings to go out and enjoy yourself with. You never told your mother about this because she would disapprove, and she always seems to be very peculiar where her lodgers are concerned. You have got along very nicely with all of them but mother always finds fault with them and ends up by turning them out. You hope this won't happen with Mr Goodman, especially as you now hope to borrow the two pounds from him. But you will have to wait for a suitable moment when you can speak to him alone. And if you have no luck with Mr Goodman, then you may even try Mrs Manning, the neighbour who often calls in to see your mother.

AT THE MOMENT you are on your way home from morning school. A thick fog has fallen which is expected to get worse, and all the pupils have been told that those who go home for lunch do not have to return for the afternoon. You will arrive home for lunch a few moments after the improvisation has begun.

Instructions for THE NEIGHBOUR

Your name is Mrs Manning and you live with your husband and three children in a semi-detached house in a London suburb. You have many friends, and you get on very well with virtually every one. You have the sort of good nature that shows friendship even to people who don't seem to want it. You have a rather strange neighbour, Mrs Brownlow, who is a widow with a young son called Wally. Mrs Brownlow has a lodger, and you're not quite sure that you approve of people having lodgers, but you don't let this interfere with your being friendly with Mrs Brownlow. After all, she is obviously a very lonely person and she needs friends. So you find all sorts of excuses for calling round on her and cheering her up. Sometimes you pretend that you want to borrow some sugar, other times that you are yourself lonely and feel like a chat and a cup of tea. But you find Mrs Brownlow rather difficult at times. And strange. For instance, only a few weeks ago she was very rude to you when you went round to invite her to join the Women's Institute, and at first she would not open the door to you. And when she eventually did open the door she started shouting at you and calling you a meddler in other people's affairs. Also she is very strange about her lodgers. She always imagines they are crooks, or men running away from their wives. And yet you have always found her lodgers very pleasant. Yes, there is definitely something odd about Mrs Brownlow and you have decided that it is high time she saw a doctor about her nerves. She might even be heading for a nervous breakdown.

AT THE MOMENT you are thinking of paying a visit to Mrs Brownlow. It is lunch-time, and even though a thick fog is falling you feel this would be a good time, for her lodger is out at work and her son is at school. You will call round at the house about three minutes after the improvisation has begun.

Instructions for THE LODGER

Your name is Peter Goodman. You are twenty-five and unmarried. You have been educated at a high school and a university and you are now trying to make a living as a writer. You have not had any great success as yet, but you have had quite a few short stories published in magazines and occasionally you write free-lance articles for newspapers. You live in lodgings in a London suburb where your landlady is a Mrs Brownlow. You pay her five guineas a week for bed and breakfast. You never tell people your real profession because you find they ask you too many questions. You have told Mrs Brownlow that you are working at the Electricity Board. You are a quiet person. You do not like to waste time. You spend most days walking around London looking for ideas to write about, and in the evenings you come home and write. Today you went out as usual, immediately after breakfast, and spent the morning walking around the City, but a dense fog has blown up and this has driven you back to your lodgings earlier than usual. You decide to tell your landlady that you have been let out of work earlier than usual because you are not feeling well. On your way home you discover that you have lost your wallet. It is quite possible that you dropped it in Mrs Brownlow's parlour when you were having breakfast, so you must ask her about it as soon as you see her. On your way there you wonder whether perhaps Mrs Brownlow's life story might not be very interesting—it might contain something that would make a good 'human interest' story for a newspaper. You must try to get her talking. You might include her son Wally in the story. He's a pleasant lad. A little while ago you gave him ten shillings as a present for himself, in order to get him away from the television set and to have a bit of quiet in the house while the landlady was out at the cinema. But it would never do to let them know that you are a writer.

AT THE MOMENT you are walking home through a thick London fog. You should reach home in about five minutes.

Instructions for ALL THE CHARACTERS
The improvisation takes place in Mrs Brownlow's house—her parlour, her front hall, and her kitchen. The layout of these three areas should be fixed, so that the characters can use each area as it is appropriate. The three areas will be closed off from each other, so that what is said in the parlour will not necessarily be heard in the kitchen, or in the hall. The characters should enter in the sequence that they have been given.

It does not matter how the story develops, nor does it need to have an actual ending. Quite often the group stops the improvisation at a certain point, the scene is discussed, and then the improvisation is continued.

Instructions for BOTH THE CHARACTERS
The scene is a bench in a London park. It is a pleasant Saturday afternoon. Richard Hart, a most ordinary-looking man, is seated at a park
bench with a newspaper in front of him. Various people pass by, but
this afternoon the park is not especially crowded. Then Paul Masters,
a slightly younger man, very smartly dressed, comes to sit on the
bench, takes a book from his pocket and starts reading. There is
silence.

Instructions for RICHARD HART
You are a bachelor of thirty, and have been employed all your working life as a salesman in a big London store. You have recently been
promoted to the position of deputy manager in the men's haber-
dashery department, and you are very pleased with this promotion.
You live with your widowed mother and your younger sister, in a
pleasant suburban house. Your sister is out at work, and you support
your mother. You have a fiancée whom you plan to marry in about
a year's time; her name is Linda, and she is a librarian. You haven't
yet worked out whether your mother will still live with you after your
marriage, or whether she will perhaps go and live with someone else.
It is possible that your sister (who is a secretary) may move into a flat
and take your mother with her. But you have never discussed this
with either your sister or your mother. You are a keen churchgoer,
and have a very strong sense of what is right, and you mean always
to do that which is right. But you are very much aware that being
right is not the same as being weak and foolish. So you do not find it
easy to forgive people who do wrong things or foolish things. You
expect other people to be like yourself—able to look after themselves
and not to make mistakes. You are constantly reading the Bible, and
find great inspiration from it.

You also have a brother—Ken, who is two years younger than yourself. Ken has always been a source of great worry to you. Unlike
yourself he has never recognised the fact that we have certain obliga-
tions to ourselves and to others. Ken has never looked after himself
properly, has never had any consideration for your mother, and has
failed to make any kind of career for himself. When he was sixteen,
Ken ran away from home—not for any reason, he wasn't unhappy or
anything like that. He just ran away. A week later you had a letter

from him, asking you to lend him the money for his train fare home. He had got as far as Liverpool and found himself broke, lonely and homesick. Mother was very upset and urged you to send him the money to come home with, and much against your better judgment, you did so. Ken never paid the money back to you. A year or two later he left home again—this time he went to sea, as a steward on a luxury liner. You all hoped he would make a success of this, and settle down to a career at sea. But a year later he ran away from his boat when it was docked in Montreal harbour, and was not heard of again for three years. Mother nearly died of a broken heart and you had definitely decided you would not hear of him again, when quite suddenly he came back. He looked much older and far from well, and had probably been living on the verge of starvation for a good few weeks, perhaps longer. Your mother welcomed him back enthusiastically, and asked you to lend him enough money to get him back on his feet. Against your better judgment you lent him £50, and he appeared to spend this sum of money almost overnight. Ken lived at home for a year or more, and never paid any rent or living expenses, and never kept a job for more than a week or two. Then one day he announced that he was going to emigrate to Canada—the land of opportunity. Frankly you couldn't see what sort of opportunities any land could offer to a man like Ken, but you said nothing. Mother got very upset over the thought of his leaving again, but he went, and was not heard of again until this morning, when a letter came addressed to your mother and yourself, and written by Ken in Vancouver. He is broke again. He has had two exciting years in Canada, and for a time, he says, was a great success and had plans to bring all the family over for a holiday, but his luck has changed, and he is near to starvation. Please, he writes, please send me the money to come home with. He declares he is a changed man, and that when he gets home he will find himself a good steady job and make a success of his life. He also declares that he has become very religious in the last few months, and wants very much to discuss all sorts of religious problems with you.

You are a fair man and very Christian. You want to help any man who really is helpless and cannot possibly help himself. But something tells you that Ken has passed the stage where anyone can help him; the only way he will ever learn his lesson is by letting him suffer the natural consequences of his acts—let him starve. Besides, you are not a rich man, far from it, your weekly wage packet is still very modest, and what you have in the bank, you got the hard way.

And you will be getting married soon, so you are no longer free to do what you would like to do with your money.

But you want to do the right thing.

Your mother and sister reckon you should send the money to Ken. But it would take at least £200 to bring Ken home. That's an awful lot of money. Your sister has offered to help, but she can hardly have more than £50 in the bank, so that wouldn't be much help.

You would welcome the chance to discuss the whole matter with someone who is quite unconnected with you and your family. You would like an independent opinion. The trouble is, you don't find it easy to talk to strangers. . . .

Instructions for PAUL MASTERS

You are twenty-two, a bachelor, and were brought up in Liverpool. Your father was, and still is, a successful solicitor. You did quite well at school, but were very keen to leave it, and so your father took you away when you were sixteen and apprenticed you as an articled clerk in his office. This meant that in five years' time or so you would yourself become a practising solicitor. You were never asked whether you wanted to be a solicitor, everybody just took it for granted that you did, and this annoyed you greatly, especially as you expected the solicitor's life to bore you mightily. In fact, you found it even more boring than you had expected. After six months of unendurable boredom you walked out of the office and out of the home. Your mother nearly had a stroke, and your father went slightly berserk, but out you walked—it could never be said that you 'ran' away from home, you just 'walked'—elegantly, and surely. You had no idea where you were going, or what you were going to do when you got there. You just went. Two weeks later you went back—still very cool, calm, and collected, but a little wiser. In the meantime you had got as far as to rent a small room for yourself, and to sign on at the Labour Exchange, and to get thoroughly depressed. After many a long talk with your parents you returned to the office, and declared that all you now wanted from life was to become a solicitor, just like father. But boredom crept in yet again. When it came to the annual exams, you not only failed, but failed quite hilariously. As mother so rightly said, 'You just aren't trying, Paul dear, are you?' But by this time you had found a new interest in life: acting. You had become the leading light of a local drama group, and were busy playing all the great rôles— Hamlet, Romeo, Jimmy Porter for instance, and all your friends and admirers were telling you that you really should go on the stage, and of course, on the films. Father, needless to say, was dead against this. So you walked out once again, moved down to London with £50 in your bank book, and went along to audition for a scholarship to the Royal Academy of Dramatic Art. You realised with a shock, when it came to the audition, that the world is full of young people who are the shining stars of their local amateur drama groups, and that vast regiments of them decide to go to drama school. You were unnecessarily nervous and you failed the audition. Deeply disappointed you returned home. You were then twenty-one—an age when, you felt, a young man should already be at least partly successful, whereas you at that age were a total failure. Your parents argued with you, but eventually you were back in father's office, where by this time you were something of a joke to all the clients and the employees. You had resolved to do no more 'dramatics'—but your local group clamoured for your services, you were cast once more in the most exciting leading rôles, and a year later you decided that you would again set forth to conquer London. But this time, you decided to do it properly, and to plan beforehand. You saved up some money, just a little, but enough to keep you decently alive for a couple of months. You also made a particular point of getting to know the right people, which meant people who could help you to become a successful actor. You met a TV director who told you you were just the sort of person who could do well in television. You met the director of your local repertory theatre, who also encouraged you. A friend of yours introduced you to the friend of a film producer, who told you to look him up when you got to London. Eventually, you told your parents of your decision, whereupon your father almost literally threw you out of the house, your mother almost literally faded away, and before you knew where you were you were in London, living in a small room in Bayswater. And that is how you are living at present. The room is rather depressing, the landlady is rather quick-tempered and theatreland is rather indifferent to your arrival. You phone up all the people who seemed as though they would help you, but they are all out, and cannot be contacted. You leave messages, but they do not answer. Your money runs out faster than you had expected. You go round all the theatrical agents, but no one is interested. You are inexperienced, and untrained—so what use are you as an actor? One agent, however, is more sympathetic than the rest, and says he may be able to help you. He takes your telephone number, and promises to ring you if a possible job should turn up. This morning, when you had almost despaired, he phoned you. He wants you to go along on Tuesday morning to meet a television director who is looking for a young man of exactly your build, accent and personality for a new television play. It is only a small part, but it is a good one. He tells you to pretend you have more experience than you actually have—a little more, at any rate. He also tells you that it is essential that you look smart. And in fact you always do look smart, you do right now, and have always taken great pride in your smart appearance. But it is doubtful whether you will still look smart when it comes to Tuesday. You have spent your last penny; you have already pawned all your clothing except for the clothes you are standing up in; you have fallen behind with your rent and unless you pay the arrears to your landlady tonight, she will throw you out. You have tried to phone your parents, but they have refused to accept the reversed charge call. You have thought of applying for National Assistance—but you doubt whether that would come through quickly enough, and at any rate the offices are closed until Monday —you don't really know what to do. You take a stroll in a nearby park. You notice this solitary figure sitting on a bench, reading the newspaper. You wonder whether the fates might suddenly be kind to you and lead you to a total stranger who has the charity to help out someone like yourself. Of course the last thing you would do would be to walk up to a total stranger and ask him to lend you £10 (though even a fiver would be a help)—but you could perhaps try to get him into conversation, and very, very slowly lead round to the possibility of a loan. You stroll up to the bench and take a seat and take a book of plays from your pocket and start reading. Very carefully you watch for a good opening gambit. . . .

A Case for the Detective

Instructions for ALL THE CHARACTERS
Earlier this evening, the Cranshaws gave a small dinner party. Eric Cranshaw has recently started work as a junior executive with Goddards Ltd, an advertising agency, and the dinner was intended to introduce himself and his wife to other members of the firm. During the dinner, conversation ranged over many topics, including a very fine diamond ring which Mrs Cranshaw was wearing. After dinner, the men smoked and drank in the dining-room while the ladies did the washing-up in the kitchen. During the washing-up the

ladies cleared everything off the dining-room table except for a vase of flowers which was left in the centre. The ladies also brought some of the crockery back into the dining-room and placed it inside the china-cabinet. Then Mrs Cranshaw screamed out that her ring was missing. The kitchen and dining-room were thoroughly searched, and then, since Mrs Cranshaw was now hysterical, Mr Cranshaw called the police. A Detective-Inspector arrives, and after ascertaining roughly what has happened he decides to interview all the members of the dinner party privately. One of the guests, Mr Cross, suggests that it would be much easier simply to have everyone searched, but the Inspector rejects this suggestion.

The layout of the ground floor is as follows: the entrance-hall leads into the dining-room and into a lounge and into a toilet; the dining-room leads into the kitchen.

Improvise the Interviews and the Inspector's Report.

The members of the dinner party are:
    Eric Cranshaw, host, aged 30.
    Ellen Cranshaw, his wife, aged 27.
    John Baldock, 55, Managing Director of Goddards Ltd.
    Kay Baldock, 50, his wife.
    Stanley Cross, 31, a Junior Executive of Goddards Ltd. A bachelor.
    Stella Larkwood, 35, spinster, assistant chief accountant at Goddards Ltd.
    Detective-Inspector.

Instructions for THE INSPECTOR
Make notes on any details that you think important. Be very polite to all the people you interview, and do not at any moment betray any suspicions that you may form. You can, if you choose, after inter- viewing everyone, ask to re-interview particular people. Your ques- tions should be designed to ascertain roughly what each person was doing at about the time the ring was stolen, and whether anything that is said conflicts significantly with other people's accounts. At the end of the interviews you should present your report, verbally, to your superiors (the rest of the group) and indicate clearly who, if at all, you consider the guilty party, and why.

You could always, of course, ask everyone to agree to being searched, but you are fully aware that by this time if anyone has stolen the ring then they would have disposed of it before you arrived. Also, all the guests have expressed a perfect willingness to co-operate with you, and this again suggests that the ring has already been disposed of. You have, however, given orders to two of your men to search the house for any signs of the ring. They conduct a very thorough search, but no ring is discovered.

Instructions for ERIC CRANSHAW

Aged thirty. Married three years. Appointed Junior Executive at Goddards three weeks ago. Your wife Ellen was very delighted with your appointment and suggested the dinner party as a way of getting to know the people you work with, and as a way of helping you to achieve promotion later on. Your wife is somewhat scatter-brained, and has already lost two rings which you bought her, though neither of those was worth very much. The insurance companies have refused to re-insure your wife's rings, and so you stand no chance of getting back the value of the missing ring, which is worth £500 and is an old family ring handed on to your wife by your own grandmother. You were enjoying the dinner party, which seemed a great success, and your first reaction when the ring was reported missing was to think that your wife had simply put it down and forgotten where. But she insists that she left it on the dining-room table before she started to do the washing-up. To do this, she must either have taken off the ring before going from the dining-room into the kitchen, or else have returned from the kitchen into the dining-room after she had cleared the dinner things away. She claims that she did it after she had actually started to wash up, and that she was advised to take the ring off by Mrs Baldock, the wife of your managing director, who like Stella Larkwood, the accountant, helped Ellen with the washing-up, while Mr Baldock, Stanley Cross (your fellow Junior Executive) and yourself sat smoking and drinking at the dining-room table. You cannot remember seeing the ring anywhere except on your wife's finger. It is not a ring that she often wears. You can remember that there was some conversation about the ring earlier in the evening. Mrs Baldock commented on it during the dinner, and everyone admired it, and Stanley Cross commented that it must be 'worth a fortune'.

You have found all your guests extremely good-humoured about this whole unfortunate business—they have been most understanding about your wife's hysterical outburst when she discovered the loss of the ring, and the Baldocks have been exceptionally kind—and so this has confirmed your belief that your wife is herself to blame, and that she has lost it, quite probably down the sink, while washing-up.

Instructions for *ELLEN CRANSHAW*

Aged twenty-seven, married three years. Husband recently appointed Junior Executive at an advertising firm, Goddards Ltd. You were delighted at this appointment, and you suggested the dinner party to him as a way of enhancing his social standing in the firm. Everyone tells you that you are rather scatter-brained, though you never quite see why. You are occasionally careless, and have in fact lost two other rings which your husband gave you, but they were not very valuable ones and you have more or less forgotten about them. Because of the loss of those two rings, both of which were insured, the insurance companies have refused to re-insure the last remaining ring, which is worth £500 and was given to you (as a family heirloom) by your husband's grandmother. You are desperate at the loss of this ring. And you remember very clearly what happened to the ring in the course of the evening:

You wore the ring for the first time in over a year, and both Mrs Baldock and Stella Larkwood (the accountant) commented on it, and admired it. Someone, one of the men probably, ventured to say that it must be worth a great deal of money. After dinner, Mrs Baldock said that she would help you with the washing-up, though you had intended to leave it until the guests had left. But Mrs Baldock insisted, and so rather than offend her —she is after all, the wife of your husband's employer—you agreed to let her help you. Stella Larkwood also said she would help you, and the three of you cleared the things into the kitchen while the men started to smoke around the table. You were already washing up when one of the women, probably Stella Larkwood, advised you not to wear the ring while you were at the sink. So as to be completely sure that the ring didn't get mixed up with the washing-up things, you went back into the dining-room and left the ring in a prominent position on the table. At that particular moment, as you remember it, the men were around the cocktail cabinet pouring out drinks and hardly noticed you. While you were washing up, both Stella Larkwood and Mrs Baldock went into the dining-room a couple of times to put various pieces of crockery into the china-cabinet.

When you went back into the dining-room and discovered that

the ring was missing, you nearly fainted. Then you became hysterical, for you were well aware that someone had taken it. You are deeply sorry that the dinner party should have ended so badly, but you are desperate to have the ring back.

You do not suspect anyone. You have found both the ladies charming, especially Mrs Baldock, and the men have been equally courteous and good-natured.

Instructions for JOHN BALDOCK

Aged fifty-five, managing director of Goddards Ltd. Married thirty years to Kay Baldock. Two children, one at school, one in the Navy. You have known for many years now that your wife is a kleptomaniac, but you love her dearly and have protected her and covered up for her with amazing skill and success. Nobody else knows. She only ever steals small things, though they are also often very valuable. Always steals things of no practical use to herself, and always loses interest in the things quite soon after stealing them. In the present instance, you and nobody else saw Mrs Cranshaw place the ring on the dining-room table just before she started to do the washing-up, and then you saw your wife a little later come in to put some crockery away in a cabinet, pick up the ring from the table and put it away in her hand-bag. At the first opportunity you went over to your wife's handbag, on a pretext of looking for a cigarette, and removed the ring. You very carefully put it back on the table.

To your astonishment, five minutes later, Mrs Cranshaw screamed out that the ring was missing.

You have no idea what could have happened. But you suspect your wife, and hope very much that she will not be found out.

You are a well-liked employer, and have the respect and goodwill of your employees. You are quite impressed with young Cranshaw, and think he will do well. You have recently helped out Stella Larkwood, the assistant accountant, with a large loan, interest free, to help out her younger brother who has got into serious financial scrapes.

Instructions for KAY BALDOCK

Aged fifty, wife of John Baldock. Married thirty years, two children, one at school, one in the Navy. Devoted to your husband, who is a brilliantly successful business man. You have for some years now suffered from an unaccountable urge to steal. Have often stolen small but valuable things for which you personally have had no use, but have never yet been found out. On the occasion in question you noticed Ellen Cranshaw's ring when you were at dinner, and commented on it, and you gathered that it was worth a great deal of money. After dinner you offered to help with the washing-up, and this gave you a golden opportunity: you advised Ellen to take the ring off while she was at the sink, saw her take it off and place it on the dining-room table, and so at the earliest opportunity you went into the dining-room to put some crockery away into the china-cabinet, saw the men pre-occupied at the drinks cabinet, and took the ring and placed it in your handbag. At least you think you did, for incredibly enough a few minutes later you saw it back again on the table, lying alongside a bowl of flowers. So you scooped up the bowl of flowers and the ring with it and placed the flowers on the china-cabinet and held the ring for the moment in the palm of your hand. You are extremely skilful at this sort of thing, and enjoy the advantage that nobody ever guesses for one instant that you could ever so much as dream of committing a crime of any kind. You go back into the kitchen just as Ellen cries out that her ring has disappeared. Realising that the situation has become dangerous you go straight into the toilet that adjoins the hall and drop the ring down the cistern and pull the chain. A few moments later you rejoin the party and express great sympathy for Ellen's predicament and suggest that she has probably left it in the kitchen.

You are a skilled liar, and have no intention that anyone should know of what you have done!

Instructions for STANLEY CROSS

Aged thirty-one. Junior Executive of Goddards Ltd for the past seven years. Bachelor. You enjoyed the dinner party and can remember the ladies chatting about the ring Mrs Cranshaw was wearing. Such things don't interest you. You remember that the ladies insisted on helping Mrs Cranshaw with the washing-up while Mr Baldock, Cranshaw and yourself poured out drinks from the cocktail cabinet in the dining-room and discussed all sorts of general topics—the world situation, golf, taxation and so on. You can remember that the women kept on popping back into the dining-room from the kitchen to put things away in the china-cabinet. You can remember only one slightly odd thing about the proceedings: at one moment Mrs Baldock, your employer's wife, a most charming lady, removed a vase of flowers from the dining-room table on to the china-cabinet, and seconds later Stella Larkwood, the highly efficient assistant accountant at your office, moved the flowers back on to the table. At about that time you heard Mrs Cranshaw screaming out that the ring was missing.

Instructions for STELLA LARKWOOD

Spinster, aged thirty-five. Assistant to the Chief Accountant at Goddards Ltd. Hard worker; well qualified. You live with your widowed mother. Have always helped your family, and recently, when your younger brother incurred a very large gambling debt, you asked your boss, Mr Baldock, if he would lend you the necessary money. He did so, and this was typical of him, for he is a most generous man, and is always willing to help people who are in difficulties. You feel a great loyalty towards him, and for this reason you never told a single person when you discovered that his wife, Mrs Baldock, is a kleptomaniac. You first made this discovery when she stole a rather attractive powder-compact from your handbag some years ago at the office. Since then you have several times seen her steal things, and on one embarrassing occasion she took you shopping with her, and proceeded to steal several quite useless items from various shop counters. On this occasion, you remember the chatter about the ring over dinner, and remember Mrs Baldock advising Mrs Cranshaw to take the ring off before doing the washing-up. When you had finished helping the two ladies with the washing-up you helped to put some of the things back into the china-cabinet, and at that moment you saw Mrs Baldock quietly scoop up the vase of flowers on the dining-room table, and you think you saw her pick up the ring which was lying alongside it. She placed the vase on the china-cabinet, and almost at that moment Mrs Cranshaw screamed out that the ring was missing. Mrs Baldock went back into the kitchen, and you guessed that she might have dropped the ring into the vase in order to rid herself of it. So you picked up the vase, almost without thinking about it, intending to look inside it, but you realised that you couldn't immediately look in the vase without attracting suspicion. So you casually put the vase down again where Mrs Cranshaw had first placed it, on the dining-room table.

You have no intention of betraying Mrs Baldock, and you realise that you are the only one who knows what has actually happened. To the best of your knowledge Mr Baldock is not aware of his wife's various thefts.

'A Very Nice Funeral'

Characters:
Harriet Jones, daughter of the deceased
Edward Jones, her husband
Tommy Jones ⎱ their sons
Graham Jones ⎰
Jack Rawlings, son of the deceased
Annie Rawlings, his wife
Ellen Rawlings, their daughter
William Rawlings, a bachelor, son of the deceased

Instructions for ALL THE CHARACTERS
Grandfather Rawlings has recently died, and the family have gathered together for a 'funeral supper' at the home of Harriet, his daughter, where he has lived for a number of years. The house is in York, and everyone knows each other: Jack's family live in a village not far away, and the two families have frequently visited each other. The exception is William Rawlings, who has not been seen in York since he came up for his mother's funeral ten years ago. None of the children remembers him, and even the adults know very little about his recent history, except that he has been living and working in London.

Instructions to HARRIET JONES
You are thirty-six and were the youngest child in your family. Your father owned a grocer's shop in a Yorkshire village, but he retired ten years ago when your mother died, and the business was handed over to your brother Jack Rawlings. At the time when the business was handed over to Jack you were rather upset, even slightly bitter, because you had expected your father to divide up the ownership of the business among his three children but in fact he did nothing of the kind. He divided it up between his two sons and left you out of it altogether. He gave as reason for this the fact that he had given you, on your marriage six years previously, the sum of £5,000 for you to buy yourself and your husband a small business of your own. With this you bought a small grocer's shop in York, but because your husband, Edward, kept on spending all the takings on dog-racing, you were eventually obliged to sell up the business, buy yourself a house, and to start going out to work. Your husband Edward appears now to have reformed, and does not any longer frequent dog-races as far

as you know; he now works as a clerk in the local government offices, and you work as a sales assistant on the cosmetics counter of a large store. You have two sons, Tommy, aged thirteen, and Graham aged eleven. You are really a very happy family. You know that you are more intelligent than your husband, and are vaguely aware that you could have married more wisely if you had only stopped to think about it at the time, but you are not the sort of person to keep on thinking about the past—'What's done cannot be undone' is your favourite epigram, and one which you never tire of quoting. Besides, you are a kind, big-hearted and generous person who has no time for regrets or for moping and complaining. You take life as it comes. Between the two of you, there is quite a fair sum of money coming into the home every week, and you have bought a good house with the money you got from the sale of the business. Your two sons are both very marvellous in your eyes, though you have a strong suspicion that the older one, Tommy, is going to be rather weak and irresponsible, like his father, while the younger one, Graham, who is a very serious and quiet young boy, has the steady shrewdness of your own side of the family.

But you have never got over the matter of your father's business. You can never understand that he should hand it over to his two sons and not give a share in it to yourself. After all, by the time he retired, your own business had come to grief and you were already working as a shop assistant. He must have realised that a share in the family business was all you needed to put you on your feet. Although your father handed over the business to both the sons, your brother William, the bachelor, never took up his share because he wanted to continue working in London as a wood-carver. But there was a firm understanding that William should be allowed to take up his share whenever he wanted to. As a result, your brother Jack has had the business all to himself for the past eight years, and as far as you can tell, he has done very nicely out of it indeed.

When your father retired, he lived first of all with brother Jack, but after a year or so he started quarrelling violently with Jack's wife, Annie, and so he moved over to York and came to live with you, and paid you a small weekly rent for a room in your house. He proved a very self-sufficient lodger, and you didn't really see a lot of him. He even did all his own cooking on a small gas ring in his room. But it was quite an inconvenience having him in the house, for in a certain way the house was no longer your own. But you never complained about this, except when the smell of cooking from his room pervaded the whole house, as it occasionally did. At any rate, you had him living with you for some nine years, while your brother would only tolerate him for one year. Every now and again you questioned your father about his reasons for not giving you a share of the business, and he always answered in the same unsatisfactory fashion—you had already been provided for. But a few months ago, when you were again discussing this with your father, he told you that he would alter his will and give you a share in the business after all. You were delighted with this, and immediately went with your father to see a solicitor, only to be told that since your father no longer owned the business, it was too late for him to give you a share in it. It was no longer his to give. To compensate you for the disappointment your father altered his will so that all his remaining capital went to you, instead of being divided equally among his three children, but since there was very little capital left—roughly £500—this did not really cheer you up very greatly. You were also very surprised that your father had so little capital left, for you thought him a rather richer man.

Now that the family are all gathered together you think it is time to discuss important matters: you have looked after your father at great cost to your family life, and at considerable inconvenience to yourself. For nine years you have provided a home for him when no one else would, and despite the fact that your father could be very difficult—he always complained that Tommy made too much noise —you never once were really unkind to him. Now, in return, you feel that Jack should take you into the family business, as a partner. But this need not involve your husband Edward, who can continue in some kind of clerical work, and who need never get anywhere near the cash register and be tempted once again to 'go to the dogs'. You reckon you would get along quite well with Jack, once you have established yourself, and although you find his wife, Annie, far too snobbish by half, you know she will soon come down from her 'high horse' once you have made your presence felt. You are determined, however, that there is to be no quarrel at the funeral supper, for that would be a dreadful discourtesy to the dead. Far from there being a quarrel, this must be a real 'family' occasion. You will even be nice to that awful little niece of yours, Jack's daughter Ellen, who is eleven years old and is so terribly 'genteel' and 'refained' that she looks and sounds as though she's liable to collapse into a heap if you so much as breathe on her. Apparently her mother never lets her play with any other children, and sends her to some awfully snobbish private school for girls only. Yes, you will even be polite, and kind, and warm-hearted to Ellen, for this is a 'family occasion'. . . .

Instructions for EDWARD JONES

You are thirty-eight, are employed as a clerk in a local government office in York, and live with your wife, Harriet, and your two children, Tommy, aged thirteen, and Graham, aged eleven, in a pleasant semi-detached house on the outskirts of the city. Your wife has dominated you ever since the day you married. It was she who was given the money by her father to buy a small business—a grocer's shop in York —and it was she who ran it and more or less compelled you to work in it as a shop assistant for no wages. And since she never paid you, you were given no alternative but to take money from the cash register from time to time, just to buy yourself a drink, or to spend the occasional shilling at the greyhound races. And when Harriet made a mess of her business, and had to sell it, she blamed you for her own failure and told the rest of her family that it was be-cause you stole so much money from the cash register that she was having to sell out. But that was nearly ten years ago, and since then your wife has been working on the cosmetics counter of a large store, and you have been employed as a clerk, and your children have started to grow up. You do not like your younger son Graham quite as much as you like Tommy, though you are immensely proud of both of them. But Graham is awfully quiet and well-behaved, while Tommy is a 'real boy', and enjoys life enormously and only occa-sionally does as he is told. Tommy is more like yourself when you were his age. You enjoy being a father, and you have learnt how to get along with your wife, letting her do a great deal of talking and shouting, and tolerating her noisiness and bossiness. For the past nine years you have had your father-in-law living with you, and you found this made life more complicated than it needed to be. 'Grand-father' was always grumbling or sulking, and although he was supposed to be living in his own room, the backroom upstairs, he spent most of his time coming into the sitting-room downstairs to complain that the TV was making too much noise, or that Tommy was making too much noise. And you knew that when he criticised Tommy he was indirectly criticising you, for everyone knows that Tommy is very much his 'father's son'. But now that grandfather is dead you will be free for ever of your wife's wretched family. Except for the occasional visit, you need never see or hear of them again. The prospect fills you with pleasure: no father-in-law, no visits from brother-in-law Jack with his snide comments about 'going to the dogs again, Edward?' or from that fearfully snobbish wife of his, Annie, and that dreadful daughter of theirs, little Ellen, who is so terribly refined she will surely have to be wrapped up in cotton wool and put under a glass case before she is much older.

You have a suspicion that your wife will inherit some money now that her father has died. She never discusses money matters with you, unless it is to make you pay for the domestic bills, and you know that you will never see any money that may come to her. So you don't intend to get too excited about that. In fact, you have no intention of getting excited about anything. You have too much common sense. But you have decided that now that the grandfather is dead and gone, you will no longer be bossed about like you used to be. You will be free of the wife's family, and will be the boss in your own house.

Instructions for *TOMMY JONES*

You are thirteen, are at a local comprehensive school, and look forward very much to joining the Royal Air Force as an apprentice flight navigator, which you will do as soon as you can leave school. Both your parents work, your father as a clerk in an office, and your mother in a store in the centre of the city. You have a younger brother, Graham, who is much more brilliant at school work than you are—you hate most of it—and who is very quiet and studious. You get along well with your father, but you find your mother a bit too much at times—she often nags about how you ought to speak, how you ought to behave, what you ought to do, and so on. You liked your grandfather who has recently died, and who lived with you, and you used to enjoy it when he talked about his earlier life and about the way people lived and worked when he was young. But he used to make a great deal of fuss whenever you had friends round, and he complained that you made too much noise. Apart from that, you were very fond of him, and thought him quite a character, and will miss him very much. You are not very fond of your Uncle Jack; he seems to be rather like your mother, and to have very strong views on the way young people should act, and you like even less your Aunt Annie, who seems to think she is the Queen of England and to look down

123

her nose at anyone like yourself. But you have always been delighted at any chance to see their daughter, your cousin Ellen, who is eleven, very refined and 'posh', and who seems more like something out of a comedy show than something out of real life. You have long experienced the strongest possible desire to say something really shocking to Ellen, just to see whether the surprise would make her fall to pieces like some delicate china figure knocked off a mantelpiece.

Instructions for *GRAHAM JONES*

You are eleven years old, are a pupil in the final year at a nearby primary school, and are looking forward to going at the end of the year to the same comprehensive school that your brother goes to. You look up to your brother as being a very clever and capable person, who can really look after himself. You do well at school and you enjoy your school-work, though you do not particularly like the games lessons or the P.E. lessons. You get along well with your father, who is easy-going and cheerful, and not quite so well with your mother, who is always encouraging you to work harder and to do even better in your tests and examinations, and who is seldom satisfied even with the good results that you produce. Your mother works in a store, your father in an office. Your grandfather also lived with you until his death last week. You got along tremendously well with him, and would sit and talk with him for hours and hours, and he was always pleased to see you and to hear your news. You also like your Uncle Jack and Aunt Annie, who always give you ten shillings when they come to see you, and you like their daughter, your cousin Ellen, who is rather shy and quiet and never seems very willing to say anything.

Instructions for *JACK* and *ANNIE RAWLINGS*

You are both forty-two years old, have been married nearly fifteen years, and have a daughter, Ellen, who is eleven. You run a grocer's shop in a small Yorkshire village, and you were given this business by Jack's father (who has just died) when he retired some ten years ago. You have done well with the business and are now interested in selling it and buying a rather larger one elsewhere. You both accept the fact that Annie is the superior half of the partnership, for she comes from a 'professional' family—her father was a solicitor's managing clerk—and her parents considered she was marrying beneath herself when she married into a family that ran a village grocery business. Annie is in fact something of a snob, and Jack is secretly proud of her for this reason, for Jack likes to feel that his wife is rather better than the neighbours, and is certainly better than his sister and her family. Neither of you approves of Jack's sister, Harriet, or of her husband Edward, or of her elder son Tommy, who is rather forward and noisy, but you have a certain respect for their younger son, Graham, who is a nice, quiet, studious boy, and you always give him ten shillings when you go to visit his family.

When 'grandfather' handed over the business to you, it was agreed that he would continue to live with you, but this didn't work out. You were both extremely kind to him, but he became very cantankerous and awkward, and he seemed to frighten your little daughter, Ellen, and so after a year or so he moved out and went to York to live with Harriet and her family. You frequently went to visit him there but you found the visits rather embarrassing because Harriet was always so unpleasant: she seemed to have the idea that you ought to let her have a share in the grocery business. This of course was sheer nonsense, for her father actually gave her the money to buy a business of her own soon after she married Edward, and apparently Edward spent all the profits at the greyhound races, and as a consequence Harriet eventually had to sell up the business and go out to work. Now Edward works as a clerk, and Harriet as a shop assistant. You cannot understand how Harriet can be so selfish as to imagine that she should have a share in your business when she has already wasted, or her husband has, the business that her father bought her. But as Annie often points out, Harriet is such a noisy, bossy type of woman, with very little tact or social know-how, that nothing she says or does will ever surprise you.

You have been surprised to learn only the other day that 'grandfather' altered his will a few months ago and left all his remaining capital to Harriet, instead of leaving it to be divided equally among all his three children. You are both furious about this. Who knows, perhaps grandfather was mentally deranged at the time he altered the will. It may perhaps be possible to challenge the validity of the will. The little money that grandfather might have left you would have come in very handy when you are looking for a new business. You are also surprised to learn that grandfather has left so little money (£500) —you had the idea that he was rather richer than he would appear to have been. Is it possible that Harriet has been secretly stealing it from him, or worse? Or has she perhaps been charging him an exorbitant rent? Or perhaps Edward has been taking money from him and spending it at the dog-races? According to Harriet, Edward is a reformed man, but you are doubtful of that.

However, this is a family occasion, and you are both decided that there should be no quarrelling at such a time as this, least of all in front of your dear Ellen, who is only eleven, and such a delicate child and so easily upset. You are both immensely fond of Ellen, and knowing how delicate she is, you do not allow her to mix with other children, and you do not, of course, send her to an ordinary school, but to a special private school for girls only, where almost all the children seem fairly nice. You are always rather worried whenever you bring Ellen to Harriet's house, because Harriet's family are not refined enough for a girl like Ellen to mix with. So you make her stay with you all the time and make sure that she doesn't say very much to her cousin Tommy, whom you consider a very noisy child, and a bad influence on anyone, especially on Ellen. You don't mind her speaking to Graham, for Graham is a nice quiet boy, but unfortunately, neither Graham nor Ellen ever has anything to say to each other.

The remaining member of the party is brother William, whom you haven't seen for many years. William is a bachelor, and is living in London where he works as a wood-carver. He has always been a stranger to the family, and no one knows much about him any more. When grandfather handed the business over to you he gave equal shares to Jack and William, but William has never taken up his share, and has left Jack to run the business on his own, so you have more or less forgotten that in strict fact the business is as much his as it is yours. And since you have worked so hard at it for so long, and he has done nothing for it whatsoever, you don't consider that it has anything to do with him any more.

Instructions for ELLEN RAWLINGS

You are eleven, and an only child. Your parents make an enormous amount of fuss of you, and never allow you out of their sight. They are convinced that you are delicate, which you are not, and will never allow you to talk to the children you would like to talk to. They send you to a private school for girls, and you loathe almost every girl in it, except for one girl whom you thought quite a character but who has recently left the school. The only bright spot in your existence has been the occasional visit to your aunt and uncle in York, where you see your cousins. Until recently your grandfather also lived with your aunt and uncle, but now he has died and you have come to a big family 'get-together' to mourn the deceased. You look forward very much to growing up, and getting free of your nagging parents, and getting out of the Yorkshire village where you live, and away from the rather dowdy grocer's shop which your parents run.

You are intrigued to see at the get-together your Uncle William, who is a bachelor of about forty, and whom you have never seen before.

Instructions for *WILLIAM RAWLINGS*

You are a bachelor of forty, and have until recently been working and living in London as a wood-carver. You are highly skilled, and have had a very good job which has paid quite well and has given you a great deal of satisfaction. But you have recently been dismissed from your work because there is simply no more demand nowadays for wood-carving, all furniture being mass-produced and 'utility'. Your father has just died, and this event has brought you back to your native Yorkshire for the first time in ten years to meet again your brother Jack, with his wife Annie and their daughter Ellen, and your sister Harriet, with her husband Edward and their two sons Tommy and Graham. Ten years ago, when your father retired, he wrote to you offering a share in the family grocery business, in partnership with your brother Jack. When you declined the offer, your father wrote to say that he had told Jack that the half-share in the business would still be yours any time you chose to take it up. You have decided that now is the time to do so. Furthermore, you have at last found the lady of your choice, a secretary in a London office, and would like to bring her back to Yorkshire with you and help you to take up your share in the family business.

You cannot remember a great deal about the lives of your various relatives over the past ten years. You can remember your sister Harriet being given a large sum of money by your father and that she spent it all on a business and then appeared to make a mess of the business and lose all the money. You know that your father was living with Harriet and her family at the time of his death. You also remember your father writing to you many years ago to say that when he died, all his three children would get a 'little nest-egg'.

You consider yourself a sensible, practical person, easy to get along with, and not quick to lose his temper or do anything silly.

AS THE SCENE BEGINS

You are all seated around the enormous table in Harriet's front parlour. Harriet is serving up the roast beef and Yorkshire pudding. . . .

A Mock Trial: R v Jackson

Characters:
  The Recorder (Judge)
  Counsel for the Prosecution
  Counsel for the Defence
  Ian Jackson, the accused
  Mrs Brandislow
  Tom Brandislow
  Mr Negulesco
  The Jury

Instructions for ALL THE CHARACTERS (*a*) THE CASE

One month ago Ian Jackson, aged eighteen, was charged at the Magistrates' Court with two larceny offences:

Stealing £10 from Mrs Brandislow on 20 January.
Stealing £10 from Mrs Brandislow on 26 February.

At the Magistrates' Court the accused pleaded Not Guilty and reserved his defence. The Prosecution witnesses, Mrs Brandislow and Tom Brandislow, gave evidence to the following effect:

Jackson and Tom Brandislow have been friends for many years. On 20 January Jackson visited Brandislow at Mrs Brandislow's house, and the two spent some time talking—about an hour—during which time Mrs Brandislow arrived home and for a short time joined in the conversation. Mrs Brandislow is a widow who runs a very successful ladies' hat shop. Tom is seventeen, and is training to be an accountant. Jackson, at the time of the first offence, was unemployed, and has spent most of his life since leaving school either out of work or changing his work. Jackson has left his parents, and lives on his own in a rented room. During the conversation between Mrs Brandislow, Tom, and Jackson, the telephone rang and Mrs Brandislow went from the sitting-room into the hall to answer the phone. At the same time,

128

Tom went into the kitchen to make a pot of tea. While she was on the phone, Mrs Brandislow wanted to refer to her diary, which was in her handbag, which she had left on the sofa in the sitting-room. She went back into the sitting-room, collected the handbag, and went back to the phone. A few moments later, while Tom was still in the kitchen, Jackson suddenly called out that he had just remembered that he had an appointment to see someone about a job, and that he would have to dash away. He said goodbye to Mrs Brandislow as he passed her in the hall. Later that evening Mrs Brandislow discovered that she had lost ten one pound notes from her handbag. Convinced that she had checked that the notes were in her bag shortly after returning home, she phoned the police. Inspector Hall visited the Brandislows, discussed the case with them, and suggested that they should carefully prepare a trap for Jackson. Following his advice, the Brandislows twice invited Jackson round for a drink and a chat during the next four weeks, and then, on 26 February, it was arranged that Jackson should again have the chance to steal the contents of the handbag. But on this occasion the money was placed there by Inspector Hall who had recorded the numbers of the notes. Jackson arrived at 6 p.m. approximately, as on the previous occasion, but this time he had been specially invited round by Tom. Jackson was now in work again—at a radio and television factory. Mrs Brandislow arrived at about 6.15 p.m. Shortly after, she went into the kitchen to make some tea, and told Tom to go into the back yard to get some coal for the fire. Jackson was thus alone in the sitting-room, with the handbag once again left on the sofa, for about three minutes. At about 7 p.m. Jackson was stopped as he was leaving the house, by Inspector Hall, who asked him to empty his pockets. From his top jacket-pocket Jackson produced the same notes which Hall had placed in Mrs Brandislow's handbag earlier that day. He was immediately charged with larceny on the two separate counts.

Jackson has no previous convictions. He pleads Not Guilty.

The layout of the house is very simple: the hall leads into the kitchen and into the sitting-room; the telephone is in the hall, and while at the telephone you cannot see into the sitting-room. The kitchen and the sitting-room are not connected.

Following the preliminary hearing in the Magistrate's Court, the case comes to the Court of Quarter Sessions for a complete hearing before a jury.

(*N.B.* Before doing this improvisation, go along to a local court of Quarter Sessions and listen to some cases. Phone the nearest police station to see if this can be arranged.

You may find it useful to place the actual scene of the crime in a house which all the improvisers know.)

(b) THE PROCEDURE IN COURT

(i) The Recorder is, as it were, the chairman as well as the Judge. All remarks must be addressed to him except where the barristers are directly addressing the Jury (as in their summings up).

(ii) The sequence of the case is as follows:

(*a*) Prisoner is charged and pleads Guilty or Not Guilty; prosecution outlines the facts of the case according to the evidence given in the Magistrates' Court by the prosecution witnesses.

(*b*) Prosecution calls and examines its witnesses and obtains from them, by means of simple and direct questions, all the facts from which the prisoner's guilt can be established.

(*c*) Defence cross-examines each of the prosecution's witnesses in order to weaken their evidence wherever possible.

(*d*) Prosecution re-examines each witness after the cross-examination, if it so chooses.

(IN THIS CASE, MRS BRANDISLOW WILL BE THE FIRST PROSECUTION WITNESS; TOM BRANDISLOW THE SECOND.

(*e*) Defence opens its case and briefly describes what it intends to do—i.e. prove the accused's innocence. Then it calls its own witnesses, in this case—THE ACCUSED, and then MR NEGULESCO. These witnesses can be cross-examined and then re-examined, just as the prosecution witnesses were.

(*f*) Defence sums up its case, and urges the Jury to return a verdict of Not Guilty.

(*g*) Prosecution sums up its case and urges the Jury to return a verdict of Guilty.

(*h*) Recorder sums up on the whole trial, reviewing the evidence in full and carefully considering it all, but without attempting to tell the Jury what their decision should be. He points out any inconsistencies or unexplained details.

(*i*) Jury retires, considers its verdict, and reaches its verdict unanimously. A jury that cannot agree after fairly exhaustive discussion is generally little more than a nuisance to everybody. Unanimous verdicts may soon be replaced by majority verdicts. This is being debated by Parliament as this book goes to press.

(*j*) The Jury returns, the Recorder asks the Foreman to announce their verdict, and the Recorder then either acquits the prisoner or proceeds to deliver sentence.

FOR THE INDIVIDUAL CHARACTERS
Ian Jackson
You are eighteen, and left school two years ago. Since then you have had a wide variety of jobs, including apprenticed electrician, assistant at a large grocery shop, assistant manager of a discothèque (which closed down, sadly enough, after only a week's existence), and bricklayer. The longest period of time you have spent in any one job is six weeks—and you have spent long periods out of work receiving unemployment benefits, and when they ran out, National Assistance. Your father is an electrician, but you have never got along with your parents and you left home when you left school, and since then you have lived in various rented rooms. In January of this year you paid an early evening visit to an old school friend of yours, Tom Brandislow, with the intention of borrowing some money from him. At that time you had been out of work for five weeks and were quite hard up. You hoped Tom would lend you £10. In the past he had often obliged with a small loan when you needed one. Tom's family is a wealthy one, and Tom is training with a very successful accountancy firm and will probably join the firm when he qualifies, so you tend to think of Tom as the one person you know who is, and always will be, well off. The only snag is that you know that his mother, a widow, disapproves of you—she thinks you are of low character and on more than one occasion in the past has accused you of being a thief. In fact you have on various occasions in your life stolen all sorts of things—usually money. At school you frequently stole any money that you found lying around, such as money left inside wallets in the gym changing-rooms, and more than once you stole the occasional five shillings or so from Tom Brandislow. No one ever suspected you except Mrs Brandislow, who seems to have been able to smell out your little acts of theft with an almost magical instinct. The reason is perfectly obvious—Mrs Brandislow is a snob, who thinks that you aren't good enough to mix with her son, and so she just dreams up any excuse she

can lay her hands on for condemning you. In fact, you have never stolen more than very small sums—and even then you have usually only stolen from people like the Brandislows who can well afford to lose the odd bit of small cash.

You arrived at the Brandislows' house at 6 p.m. on Tuesday, 20 January. Tom had just arrived home, but Mrs Brandislow, as you expected, was not yet home. You did not tell Tom the real purpose for your visit. You told him you just wanted to hear how he was, and how the world was treating him. You sat chatting with him in the sitting-room for a short time. He was not especially friendly, though he was polite. Then his mother arrived home, was obviously not pleased to see you, but in a rather formal fashion sat chatting with you for five minutes or so. Then she left the room to answer the telephone, leaving her handbag on the sofa. Almost simultaneously Tom went into the kitchen to make some tea. Knowing that Mrs Brandislow is the sort of person who always carries money around, you first made quite sure that she was still engaged on the phone, and that Tom would be out of the room for a few minutes, and then went over to the handbag, opened it, opened the purse inside the handbag, and removed £10 in notes. The whole operation took only a minute, and it was finished not a second too soon for almost before you had replaced the handbag Mrs Brandislow rushed into the room, picked up the handbag and returned to the phone. Deciding not to push your luck any further you called out to Tom that you had suddenly remembered an appointment about a vacant job, and calling good-bye to Mrs Brandislow, left the house. Only a few minutes previously you had told Tom that you would join him and his mother for a cup of tea, and that you had no plans for that evening.

A week later, Tom invited you round again. You were aware that this might be some kind of trap, and so you decided you would definitely neither steal nor borrow on this occasion. This time you were invited round for dinner. You were invited round again a week later—and again you were on your best behaviour—and again on 26 February. By this time you were back in work, at a radio and television factory. This is not your sort of work at all, but it will do for the time being. On 26 February Mrs Brandislow again left the room to answer the phone, and Tom left the room to fetch some coal. The handbag was left as before, on the sofa. Once again you opened it, opened the purse inside, found £10, took it and pocketed it, and then, when the Brandislows came back into the room carefully waited for your chance to leave. Some fifteen minutes later you remembered that you had to go and see your mother, and you left. No sooner had you walked out through the garden gate than Inspector Hall stopped you, asked you to empty your pockets, which you did, and you were immediately charged with stealing the money from Mrs Brandislow on the two separate occasions.

You are pleading Not Guilty, and reckon that you have a good chance of being acquitted. You have invented a remarkable network of lies which you think cannot fail to deceive the Jury. This is the story which you will tell your barrister and the court:

Mrs Brandislow has always been against you. Has often accused you of theft, and yet everyone knows that you are an absolutely honest person. You have a perfectly clean record, and have never broken the law in your life and never will do so. On the occasion of the first alleged offence, you stole nothing. You went around to chat, talked with both Tom and his mother, and then left when you remembered an interview you were supposed to have about a job. (If pressed for details of this interview you will say that it was for a job which you had seen advertised in the evening newspaper but that when you left the Brandislows you discovered you had lost the paper and were not able to buy another one until it was too late to go along for the interview.)

As regards the second offence your story to the barrister and court will be as follows: you went around at the invitation of Mrs Brandislow and Tom. On entering the house you hung up your jacket in the hall near the telephone (in fact you did nothing of the kind; it was a cold day, and you only took your overcoat off). In the course of the visit, Mrs Brandislow left the room to answer the telephone, taking her handbag with her. Later you left the house in order to go to the cinema and were immediately arrested by the Inspector, who found the money in your top jacket-pocket. You will suggest to the barrister that Mrs Brandislow placed the notes in your top pocket while you were sitting innocently in the sitting-room, and while you thought she was still answering the phone. You have found a perfect witness to help you substantiate your version of what happened—Mr Negulesco.

Mr Negulesco is the manager of a large grocer's shop—Good Foods Ltd—where you worked about one year ago for six weeks as an assistant. He thought you a very bright and capable young man and when you left him, he gave you an excellent testimonial and told you that he would always be pleased to re-employ you. Ironically enough, he never discovered that you regularly stole small sums of money from his cash register. On one occasion Mrs Brandislow entered the shop and was surprised to see you working there. Mr Negulesco later told you that Mrs Brandislow took him aside shortly afterwards to warn him that you were a dishonest young man and that he ought to keep a careful check on any cash registers that you might have access to. Mr Negulesco told her that he had great trust in you and that you were proving a model employee. Mrs Brandislow said that she was pleased to hear it, and although she had been a regular customer there up to that time, never visited the shop again. Recently you visited Mr Negulesco, gave him your version of what has happened and asked him if he would be willing to appear as a witness on your behalf to tell the court what a good employee you were, and to tell how Mrs Brandislow, even a year ago, was going around accusing you of being a thief, and trying to wreck your career. When the court hears all this you are convinced that the Jury will begin to doubt the truth of the charges against you. Since you were genuinely asking Mr Negulesco to tell the truth he readily agreed to give evidence.

You will not tell the barrister or the court anything which you feel may be damaging to your case.

Mr Negulesco

You are the manager of a large grocer's shop—Good Foods Ltd. A year ago the accused in this case, Ian Jackson, then aged seventeen, came to work for you as a shop assistant. He worked well, you found him bright and conscientious and you would have liked to keep him in your employ but unfortunately he left you after only six weeks to take up a job elsewhere. You were sorry to lose him and told him that you would always be pleased to re-employ him.

An unusual incident occurred while he was in your employ. One of your regular customers, Mrs Brandislow, a wealthy business woman, told you that she knew Jackson very well as he was a friend of her son. She warned you that Jackson was secretly a thief and was virtually a kleptomaniac—i.e. someone quite unable to stop himself stealing. She added that the boy has no moral scruples and will lie his way out of any situation that may arise. You thanked her politely for the warning but added that you found Jackson a model employee and could not for one moment believe that he would ever steal anything. You said that you would certainly keep a lookout for any thefts while Jackson was around, but in fact no such theft ever occurred to the best of your knowledge while Jackson was in the shop. Privately you decided that Mrs Brandislow was insane, and you reported the whole incident to Jackson who, like yourself, was highly amused by it. Mrs Brandislow never again visited the shop.

You have now been visited by Jackson who has told you that Mrs Brandislow has dreamed up an elaborate set of accusations against him and these have landed him in court. He has asked you if you will testify to the court that he worked with you, and that he was honourable and reliable. He has also asked you to relate to the court the whole episode of Mrs Brandislow's conversation with you. Since all this is the perfect truth, you have readily agreed.

Tom Brandislow
No additional information to the general instructions for all the characters, apart from the following:

You think Jackson is quite a pleasant fellow, and find it hard to believe that he could steal.

You know your mother has always had it in for Jackson.

You disliked immensely the whole idea of trapping Jackson, and are enormously surprised that the trap actually worked.

You are convinced that Jackson stole the second lot of money, even if there is still some doubt about the first lot.

You remember all the facts very clearly, but you cannot quite recall whether Jackson, on the occasion when the second offence was committed, took his overcoat off in the hall and hung it in the wardrobe in the hall, or whether he took it off in the sitting-room and left it over one of the chairs.

Mrs Brandislow
No additional information, except for the following:

You have always disliked Jackson; you have always known he is dishonest; even when Tom and he were at school together you were convinced that he was the one who kept on stealing sums of money from Tom's pockets.

You have never failed to warn people of the sort of person Jackson is; you always have been a blunt person, and you believe in saying

135

what you believe; that is why you have succeeded in the business world; a year ago, when Jackson was working at Good Foods Ltd, you told the manager, Mr Negulesco, that Jackson was a thief but the man was too stupid to take your advice, and so you decided to buy your groceries elsewhere. Strangely enough, no one has ever listened to your advice, not even your own son, Tom, who still believes that Jackson is quite a good fellow.

Your recollection of the facts of the case is completely fool-proof. As regards the second occasion, the only point you are not absoutely clear about is whether Jackson left his overcoat in the wardrobe in the hall, or whether he took it off in the sitting-room and left it over one of the chairs. Apart from this you have a complete mental picture of everything that happened on both occasions.

For Improvisation
First the defence counsel should interview the prisoner, in order to collect in detail his version of the facts. This interview must of course be in the absence of *all* the other characters. In an actual case it would take place in a special room in the court house, perhaps only shortly before the case is heard. Quite often the barrister does not himself interview the prisoner at all—this is done by a solicitor, who then prepares a dossier/brief which is given to the barrister.
Then improvise the court case.

IV

Improvisation as a way of studying a literary text or producing and rehearsing a play

IV Improvisation as a way of studying a literary text or producing and rehearsing a play

When an actor is rehearsing a play, and when a student is studying a play for examination purposes, he must acquire great familiarity with his text. The style of the play, the characters in it, its dramatic development—all these must become clear and vivid in his mind. It is in the process of making a text 'vivid' and 'vital' that improvisation can play an important part. Very often, studying a play with a view to taking an examination, means little more than taking notes on difficult parts of the text, and writing a series of essays. Similarly, many plays are produced without attempting to bring the actor to an imaginative involvement in the rôle he is playing or in the play itself. Improvisation can never be a substitute for detailed textual study, it can only help to illuminate the study, to lift the play off the printed page and to make it a piece of genuine drama. Similarly, improvisation is not the same thing as 'production'—even if you get your actors to do a great deal of improvising, they will still need to be 'produced', to be given moves, to be helped with all the various technical problems which acting involves, and to have each individual performance moulded into a single 'production'.

In what ways can improvisation help the student and the actor?—It can:

(i) Clarify the story-line and the dramatic development of the plot.
(ii) Increase one's understanding of the characters.
(iii) Develop an understanding of the historical period in which the play takes place and of the style of the play.

The technique is roughly this:
Read a scene through.
Talk about the story and agree upon a summarised account of it.
Take the story in short episodes and improvise each episode in various ways; first, take the situation and give short improvisations in which the situation is handled in different ways and with differing characters; when you have fully painted the situation, then:

139

Talk about the characters involved in the episode; improvise the situation using the characters of the playwright as you understand them; follow the writer's development of the plot but use your own language; where there is disagreement about the interpretation of a character, or the meaning of a particular line, improvise around all the possible interpretations.

Piece together all the information which the writer gives you on each character; do some research into the social history of the period; then ask each person to choose one character on whom he answers questions from the others—questions about his background, upbringing, schooling, work, wife, children, opinions, travels and religion.

Improvise events which are referred to in the scene but which are not actually presented; improvise the events leading up to a character's entrance and following his exit.

Discuss the ways in which the scene might have been written by other writers at other times; perhaps improvise the scene as it might be handled in other theatrical styles.

Improvisation can be used for the study of any kind of literature. Two examples are given here. The first from a play (*The Merchant of Venice*) and the second from Jane Austen's novel, *Northanger Abbey*. Read the texts through and then look at the exercises on the texts.

Extract from *The Merchant of Venice* by William Shakespeare.

Act I

Scene I. Venice

Enter Antonio, Salarino, and Solanio.

Antonio In sooth I know not why I am so sad,
  It wearies me: you say it wearies you;
  But how I caught it, found it, or came by it,
  What stuff 'tis made of, whereof it is born,
  I am to learn: and such a want-wit sadness makes of me
  That I have much ado to know myself.
Solanio Your mind is tossing on the Ocean,
  There where your Argosies with portly sail[1]
  Like Signiors and rich burghers on the flood,
  Or as it were the pageants of the sea,
  Do over-peer the petty traffickers
  That curtsy to them, do them reverence
  As they fly by them with their woven wings.

Salarino Believe me sir, had I such venture forth,
   The better part of my affections would
   Be with my hopes abroad. I should be still
   Plucking the grass to know where sits the wind,
   Peering in maps for ports, and piers, and roads:
   And every object that might make me fear
   Misfortune to my ventures, out of doubt
   Would make me sad.
Solanio My wind cooling my broth,
   Would blow me to an ague, when I thought
   What harm a wind too great might do at sea.
   I should not see the sandy hour-glass run,
   But I should think of shallows, and of flats,
   And see my wealthy *Andrew* dock'd in sand,
   Vailing her high top lower than her ribs
   To kiss her burial; should I go to church
   And see the holy edifice of stone,
   And not bethink me straight of dangerous rocks,
   Which touching but my gentle vessel's side
   Would scatter all her spices on the stream,
   Enrobe the roaring waters with my silks,
   And in a word, but even now worth this,
   And now worth nothing. Shall I have the thought
   To think on this, and shall I lack the thought
   That such a thing bechanc'd would make me sad?
   But tell not me, I know Antonio
   Is sad to think upon his merchandise.
Antonio Believe me no, I thank my fortune for it,
   My ventures are not in one bottom trusted,
   Nor to one place; nor is my whole estate
   Upon the fortune of this present year:
   Therefore my merchandise makes me not sad.
Solanio Why then you are in love.
Antonio Fie, fie.
Solanio Not in love neither: then let us say you are sad
   Because you are not merry; and 'twere as easy
   For you to laugh and leap, and say you are merry
   Because you are not sad. Now by two-headed Janus,[2]
   Nature hath fram'd strange fellows in her time:
   Some that will evermore peep through their eyes,

And laugh like parrots at a bag-piper.
And other of such vinegar aspect,
That they'll not show their teeth in way of smile,
Though Nestor swear the jest be laughable.[3]

Enter Bassanio, Lorenzo, and Gratiano.

Solanio   Here comes Bassanio, your most noble kinsman,[4]
Gratiano, and Lorenzo. Fare ye well,
We leave you now with better company.
Salarino   I would have stay'd till I had made you merry,
If worthier friends had not prevented me.
Antonio   Your worth is very dear in my regard.
I take it your own business calls on you,
And you embrace th' occasion to depart.
Solanio   Good morrow my good Lords.
Bassanio   Good signiors both, when shall we laugh? say, when?
You grow exceeding strange: must it be so?
Solanio   We'll make our leisures to attend on yours.

Exeunt Salarino and Solanio.

Lorenzo   My Lord Bassanio, since you have found Antonio
We two will leave you, but at dinner-time
I pray you have in mind where we must meet.
Bassanio   I will not fail you.
Gratiano   You look not well Signior Antonio,
You have too much respect upon the world:
They lose it that do buy it with much care,
Believe me you are marvellously chang'd.
Antonio   I hold the world but as the world Gratiano,
A stage, where every man must play a part,
And mine a sad one.
Gratiano   Let me play the fool,
With mirth and laughter let old wrinkles come,
And let my liver rather heat with wine,
Than my heart cool with mortifying groans.
Why should a man whose blood is warm within,
Sit like his grandsire, cut in alabaster?
Sleep when he wakes? and creep into the jaundice
By being peevish? I tell thee what Antonio,
I love thee, and it is my love that speaks:
There are a sort of men, whose visages

Do cream and mantle like a standing pond,
And do a wilful stillness entertain,
With purpose to be dress'd in an opinion
Of wisdom, gravity, profound conceit,
As who should say, I am Sir Oracle,
And when I ope my lips, let no dog bark.[5]
O my Antonio, I do know of these
That therefore only are reputed wise,
For saying nothing; when I am very sure
If they should speak, would almost dam those ears
Which hearing them would call their brothers fools:
I'll tell thee more of this another time.
But fish not with this melancholy bait
For this fool gudgeon, this opinion:[6]
Come good Lorenzo, fare ye well awhile,
I'll end my exhortation after dinner.

Lorenzo   Well, we will leave you then till dinner time.
I must be one of these same dumb wise men,
For Gratiano never lets me speak.

Gratiano   Well, keep me company but two years mo,
Thou shalt not know the sound of thine own tongue.

Antonio   Fare you well, I'll grow a talker for this gear.[7]

Gratiano   Thanks i' faith, for silence is only commendable
In a neat's tongue dried, and a maid not vendible.[8]

Exeunt Gratiano and Lorenzo.

Antonio   It is that anything now.[9]

Bassanio   Gratiano speaks an infinite deal of nothing, more than any
man in all Venice, his reasons are as two grains of wheat hid in
two bushels of chaff: you shall seek all day ere you find them, and
when you have them they are not worth the search.

Antonio   Well: tell me now, what Lady is the same
To whom you swore a secret pilgrimage
That you today promis'd to tell me of?

Bassanio   'Tis not unknown to you Antonio
How much I have disabled mine estate,
By something showing a more swelling port
Than my faint means would grant continuance:[10]
Nor do I now make moan to be abridg'd[11]
From such a noble rate, but my chief care

Is to come fairly off from the great debts
Wherein my time something too prodigal
Hath left me gag'd: to you Antonio
I owe the most in money, and in love,
And from your love I have a warranty
To unburthen all my plots and purposes,
How to get clear of all the debts I owe.

Antonio I pray you good Bassanio let me know it.
And if it stand as you yourself still do,
Within the eye of honour, be assur'd
My purse, my person, my extremest means
Lie all unlock'd to your occasions.

Bassanio In my school days, when I had lost one shaft
I shot his fellow of the selfsame flight
The selfsame way, with more advised watch
To find the other forth, and by adventuring both,
I oft found both.[12] I urge this childhood proof,
Because what follows is pure innocence.
I owe you much, and like a wilful youth,
That which I owe is lost: but if you please
To shoot another arrow that self way
Which you did shoot the first, I do not doubt,
As I will watch the aim, or to find both,
Or bring your latter hazard back again,
And thankfully rest debtor for the first.[13]

Antonio You know me well, and herein spend but time
To wind about my love with circumstance,
And out of doubt you do me now more wrong
In making question of my uttermost[14]
Than if you had made waste of all I have:
Then do but say to me what I should do
That in your knowledge may by me be done,
And I am prest unto it: therefore speak.

Bassanio In Belmont is a Lady richly left,
And she is fair, and fairer than that word,
Of wondrous virtues, sometimes from her eyes
I did receive fair speechless messages:
Her name is Portia, nothing undervalu'd
To Cato's daughter, Brutus' Portia,[15]
Nor is the wide world ignorant of her worth,

For the four winds blow in from every coast
Renowned suitors, and her sunny locks
Hang on her temples like a golden fleece,
Which makes her seat of Belmont Colchos' strond,[16]
And many Jasons come in quest of her.
O my Antonio, had I but the means
To hold a rival place with one of them,
I have a mind presages me such thrift,[17]
That I should questionless be fortunate.
Antonio Thou know'st that all my fortunes are at sea,
Neither have I money, nor commodity
To raise a present sum, therefore go forth
Try what my credit can in Venice do,
That shall be rack'd even to the uttermost,
To furnish thee to Belmont to fair Portia.
Go presently inquire, and so will I
Where money is, and I no question make
To have it of my trust, or for my sake.

Exeunt.

Textual Notes

1 There where your Argosies . . . i.e. where your ships sail along majestically looking like wealthy citizens or giant models dressed up for a carnival, and peering down at all the little ships that tip and bobble in their wake.
2 *Janus* a two-headed God, one was smiling, the other frowning.
3 *Nestor* a grave and venerable Greek commander; if even he thought a joke was funny, then it must be very funny indeed.
4 *Kinsman* in fact, such a relationship between Bassanio and Antonio is never again referred to.
5 i.e. some people use silence as a means of impressing others with the idea that they are wise.
6 i.e. only a fool could think people are clever when they are only silent, so don't waste your time trying to impress fools. (Gudgeon =bait.)
7 *Gear* purpose.
8 i.e. in a tongue ready for eating or in an old maid.
9 i.e. Gratiano's silence would be most welcome right now.
10 i.e. by living beyond my means.

11 i.e. and I am not moaning now about having to cut down my style of living.

12 A rather complicated idea—roughly: As a schoolboy, when I lost one arrow I would use another arrow to find it with, for since both had equal power there was a good chance that by following carefully the flight of the second, it would lead me to the first.

13 i.e. I will either be able to pay off both the debts or at least will be able to return the second loan and continue to owe you the first.

14 i.e. you do me wrong to question that I would do my utmost to help you.

15 Portia was the noble wife of Brutus and daughter of Cato.

16 Colchos' strond—it was from Colchos that the Golden Fleece was taken by Jason; *strond*—strand or strip of beach.

17 i.e. I anticipate such profit.

Exercises

1 Discuss what happens in this scene. List the main episodes.

2 What kind of play does the very opening speech of *The Merchant* lead you to expect?

3 In the opening sequence, Antonio confesses that he is sad and that he does not know why; Solanio and Salarino then proceed to remove his melancholy by showing the possible causes of it. (Would you agree with this as an explanation of Salarino's or Solanio's opening speeches?) What are the possible causes that they suggest?

4 Improvise the following scene, with variations: You are travelling home from work; you meet a friend and start chatting; you realise he is depressed; you try to cheer him up. . . . Improvise the scene, imagining first that the two characters are great friends, then that they are polite acquaintances, and then that they are privately distrustful of each other. Then improvise with an additional character. . . . In what ways does the scene change when there are more than two present?

5 Improvise the same scene, but this time change the status of each

character. For instance, make the depressed person the employer of the others; and then reverse this. In what ways does this affect the basic situation?

6 What do we learn about Antonio from the opening sequence between Solanio, Salarino and himself?

7 Why does Antonio say so little in the opening sequence? What, if anything, does his relative silence suggest? Judging from the remainder of the scene, how far is his silence typical of him?

8 Re-write the speeches of Solanio and Salarino in modern idiomatic English. How would you describe their style of speaking to Antonio? What does it suggest of their relationship with him? Do they speak at great length or with economy? Are they assured or hesitant? Do they appear sincere?

9 Briefly improvise these scenes:

A plumber and his mate are repairing a water tank in someone's loft; the mate is miserable and hasn't much to say for himself; the plumber can't stand a miserable mate. . . .

The Duchess of Frumpington is being driven along in her Rolls-Royce to open the Frumpingtonshire Cattle Show. She is extremely depressed, for she is allergic to cattle, and though she has opened the show every year for as long as she can remember she always finds the occasion a most miserable one. But she has a strong sense of duty and refuses to confess to anyone that she doesn't like doing any of her many jobs. Being depressed she gets very irritated when her car is caught up in various traffic jams. Her Lady-in-Waiting, the Honourable Mrs Willoughby-Smith, carefully attempts to cheer her up. . . .

Two stock-brokers are travelling home by train; they've had a hard day; one of them has just risked his entire fortune on a business venture that may or may not come off; the other one knows this and presumes that this accounts for his silence this evening; he attempts to cheer him up. . . .

10 Are there any indications in the text as to what is happening during the opening dialogue? What are the three characters actually doing? How would you produce this scene on a stage?

11 Is there any difference between the account that Antonio gives to Salarino and Solanio of his current business affairs and the account he gives Bassanio? Does the difference, if any, have a significance?

12 Could the characters of Salarino and Solanio be presented as

147

basically unfriendly towards Antonio? What parts of the text would lend weight to such a portrayal, and what parts would make such a portrayal difficult?

13 Why do Solanio and Salarino leave as soon as Bassanio and the others appear?

14 Try performing the short sequence from the entrance of Bassanio and the others to the exit of Solanio and Salarino in the following ways:

All the men are extremely affable and friendly towards each other, but Solanio and Salarino know that Bassanio and Antonio will want to speak privately with each other.

Solanio and Salarino are merchants, like Antonio, but are of lower status than Antonio, and need to stay in his good books and to ingratiate themselves with him, since his good opinion may one day be of great use to them; they meet Antonio one day at their club, or perhaps in a café, and though they wish to talk business between themselves, they think it wise to stay and talk with him; they get away at the first opportunity—when friends of Antonio appear on the scene.

The same as before, except that this time Salarino and Solanio are business rivals of Bassanio and the others.

The same as before, except that this time Salarino and Solanio are envious of Bassanio's friendship with the influential Antonio, and they show their dislike to Bassanio but hide it from Antonio. Do any of these versions appear to make sense with the text? What other possible variations are there?

15 Is there any special significance in the fact that Antonio explains why Solanio and Salarino are going?

16 What are the possible implications of the line 'when shall we laugh?' Does it necessarily mean any more than a pleasantry?

17 Bassanio says, 'You grow exceeding strange' just before Solanio and Salarino depart. There are various ways of playing this short sequence. Explore them.

18 Is there any evidence in the remainder of the scene that Antonio or Bassanio know Solanio and Salarino well?

19 Would the scene be any less effective if the opening dialogue between Antonio, Salarino and Solanio were cut, and the play began with the arrival of Bassanio and the others?

20 What is the purpose of the visit of Bassanio and the others?

21 Why does Gratiano not leave as soon as Lorenzo offers to leave?

22 From Gratiano's attempt to cheer up Antonio what do we learn about Antonio that we did not learn from the earlier sequence?

23 List the various arguments that Gratiano employs. In what ways, if at all, do they vary from the earlier arguments?

24 What possible differences in their lives and occupations are suggested by the arguments of Gratiano and Solanio?

25 What is the general feeling about Gratiano? Is he disliked?

26 What principal event does the scene build towards?

27 Improvise the following: You have a wealthy friend, who has often, in the past, helped you out with loans, most of which you have never repaid. He has never pressed you for the repayments, and the friendship is still a firm one. You need more money, this time because you have the chance of making such a fortune that you could pay off all your old debts and still have a fortune left for yourself—but you need one more loan before you can take advantage of the opportunity. You visit your old friend. . . .

28 Improvise the same scene, but this time you expect very great difficulty, for you have learnt that your friend, although basically still a rich man, has recently invested his fortune in a somewhat shaky business venture which may quite possibly collapse. So you know that it will be very important to the friend that he should only make loans where he knows quite definitely that he will get the money back. . . .

29 Briefly improvise the following:
A young boy trying to borrow five shillings from his father so that he can go to the pictures; father disapproves of the pictures, but the boy is a skilful pleader.
The same boy trying to borrow the money from his mother, who is much more lenient with the boy than the father is, but she has been told by the father that the boy is not to be given the money.
A business man trying to borrow money from a wealthy colleague for an ambitious and rather risky business venture.
Looking back on all these improvisations, what techniques are commonly employed by people when they want to borrow something? How direct are they in their approach? How honest?— Now ask these questions in relation to Bassanio's request for another loan from Antonio.

30 Is Antonio surprised at the request?

31 Bassanio gives quite a long-winded build-up to the request for a loan. Put it into simple idiomatic English. He then says, that he

has talked about his schooldays in this fashion because 'what follows is pure innocence'. What does he actually mean by this? Is it in fact 'pure innocence'?

32 Why does Bassanio not talk straight away about the Lady in Belmont? Why does he not immediately answer Antonio's first question to him?

33 Improvise the following: You have recently seen a most beautiful girl, whom you are determined to get to know better, and whom you already think you would like to marry. Talk about it with a friend. Improvise the scene in various settings and with very varied people.

34 From the improvisations: How do people tend to talk about someone they are immensely attracted to? In what order do they tend to list their qualities? In what order does Bassanio list the qualities of his Lady? Is there any significance in this order?

35 Could the scene be played in such a way as to suggest that Bassanio is interested in the Lady mainly and perhaps only for her money? Could he at the same time be presented as a sympathetic character?

36 Consider the period in which the play takes place, and the kind of society with which it is dealing. Would it be considered wrong in those days for a young man to expect financial profit to come from his marriage? Would it be unusual or wrong for a man to marry for such a reason in your own society today?

37 Is it possible to play the short sequence where Bassanio lists the Lady's virtues in such a way as to suggest that he puts her least virtue first and then proceeds to the more important ones?

38 Bassanio speaks of the Lady's 'sunny locks' as hanging 'on her temples like a golden fleece'. The expression 'golden fleece' was often used in Shakespeare's time as a metaphor for the fortunes which all merchants hoped to gain. Is there any significance in this?

39 Quite a lot of words are showered on Antonio by his friends, first to cheer him up, and secondly to get money from him. Do they appear to have been necessary?

40 By the end of the scene, have we learnt why Antonio is unhappy? Is he any happier? Do we expect his unhappiness to be resolved in the course of the play? Which characters do we expect to see more of in the next scenes, and how do we expect the story to develop?

Extract from *Northanger Abbey* by Jane Austen

[At the age of seventeen, Catherine Morland, a clergyman's daughter, is brought to Bath by some friends of her parents. At this time—very early nineteenth century—Bath is the centre of England's social life, but Catherine's first few days in the city prove uneventful until she meets Isabella Thorpe, who is four years her senior, very good-looking, and apparently well-versed in the ways of the world. As for Catherine herself—'her heart was affectionate; her disposition cheerful and open, without conceit or affectation of any kind; her manners just removed from the awkwardness and shyness of a girl; her person pleasing, and, when in good looks, pretty; and her mind about as ignorant and uninformed as the female mind at seventeen usually is.']

The following conversation, which took place between the two friends in the Pump Room one morning, after an acquaintance of eight or nine days, is given as a specimen of their very warm attachment, and of the delicacy, discretion, originality of thought, and literary taste which marked the reasonableness of that attachment.

They met by appointment; and as Isabella had arrived nearly five minutes before her friend, her first address naturally was—'My dearest creature, what can have made you so late? I have been waiting for you at least this age!'

'Have you indeed? I am very sorry for it, but really I thought I was in very good time. It is but just one. I hope you have not been here long?'

'Oh! these ten ages, at least. I am sure I have been here this half-hour. But now, let us go and sit down at the other end of the room, and enjoy ourselves. I have a hundred things to say to you. In the first place, I was so afraid it would rain this morning, just as I wanted to set off; it looked very showery, and that would have thrown me into agonies. Do you know, I saw the prettiest hat you can imagine in a shop window in Milsom Street just now—very like yours, only with coquelicot ribands instead of green; I quite longed for it. But, my dearest Catherine, what have you been doing with yourself all this morning? Have you gone on with *Udolpho*?'

'Yes, I have been reading it ever since I woke; and I am got to the black veil.'

'Are you indeed? How delightful! Oh, I would not tell you what is behind the black veil for the world! Are not you wild to know?'

'Oh! yes, quite; what can it be? But do not tell me. I would not be told upon any account. I know it must be a skeleton; I am sure it is Laurentina's skeleton. Oh, I am delighted with the book! I should like to spend my whole life reading it, I assure you; if it had not been to meet you, I would not have come away from it for all the world.'

'Dear creature, how much I am obliged to you! and when you have finished *Udolpho*, we will read *The Italian* together; and I have made out a list of ten or twelve more of the same kind for you.'

'Have you indeed? How glad I am! What are they all?'

'I will read you their names directly. Here they are, in my pocket-book: *Castle of Wolfenbach, Clermont, Mysterious Warnings, Necromancer of the Black Forest, Midnight Bell, Orphan of the Rhine*, and *Horrid Mysteries*. Those will last us some time.'

'Yes, pretty well; but are they all horrid? are you sure they are all horrid?'

'Yes, quite sure; for a particular friend of mine, a Miss Andrews, a sweet girl, one of the sweetest creatures in the world, has read every one of them. I wish you knew Miss Andrews; you would be delighted with her. She is netting herself the sweetest cloak you can conceive. I think her as beautiful as an angel, and I am so vexed with the men for not admiring her. I scold them all amazingly about it.'

'Scold them! Do you scold them for not admiring her?'

'Yes, that I do. There is nothing I would not do for those who are really my friends. I have no notion of loving people by halves; it is not my nature. My attachments are always excessively strong. I told Captain Hunt at one of our assemblies this winter that if he was to tease me all night I would not dance with him unless he would allow Miss Andrews to be as beautiful as an angel. The men think us incapable of real friendship, you know; and I am determined to show them the difference. Now, if I were to hear anybody speak slightingly of you, I should fire up in a moment; but that is not at all likely, for *you* are just the kind of girl to be a great favourite with the men.'

'Oh dear!' cried Catherine, colouring; 'how can you say so?'

'I know you very well: you have so much animation, which is exactly what Miss Andrews wants; for I must confess there is something amazingly insipid about her. Oh! I must tell you that, just after we parted yesterday, I saw a young man looking at you so earnestly, I am sure he is in love with you.' Catherine coloured, and disclaimed again. Isabella laughed. 'It is very true, upon my honour; but I see how it is: you are indifferent to everybody's admiration, except that of one gentleman, who shall be nameless. Nay, I cannot blame you' (speaking more seriously), 'your feelings are easily understood. Where the heart is really attached, I know very well how little one can be pleased with the attention of anybody else. Everything is so insipid, so uninteresting, that does not relate to the beloved object! I can perfectly comprehend your feelings.'

'But you should not persuade me that I think so very much about Mr Tilney, for perhaps I may never see him again.'

'Not see him again! My dearest creature, do not talk of it. I am sure you would be miserable if you thought so.'

'No, indeed; I should not. I do not pretend to say that I was not very much pleased with him; but while I have *Udolpho* to read, I feel as if nobody could make me miserable. Oh, the dreadful black veil! My dear Isabella, I am sure there must be Laurentina's skeleton behind it.'

'It is so odd to me that you should never have read *Udolpho* before; but I suppose Mrs Morland objects to novels.'

'No, she does not. She very often reads *Sir Charles Grandison* herself; but new books do not fall in our way.'

'*Sir Charles Grandison!* That is an amazing horrid book, is it not? I remember Miss Andrews could not get through the first volume.'

'It is not like *Udolpho* at all; yet I think it is very entertaining.'

'Do you indeed? You surprise me. I thought it had not been readable. But, my dearest Catherine, have you settled what to wear on your head to-night? I am determined, at all events, to be dressed exactly like you. The men take notice of *that* sometimes, you know.'

'But it does not signify if they do,' said Catherine very innocently.

'Signify! O heavens! I make it a rule never to mind what they say. They are very often amazingly impertinent, if you do not treat them with spirit, and make them keep their distance.'

'Are they? Well, I never observed *that*. They always behave very well to me.'

'Oh! they give themselves such airs. They are the most conceited creatures in the world, and think themselves of so much importance! By-the-bye, though I have thought of it a hundred times, I have always forgot to ask you what is your favourite complexion in a man. Do you like them best dark or fair?'

'I hardly know. I never much thought about it. Something between both, I think: brown—not fair, and not very dark.'

'Very well, Catherine. That is exactly he. I have not forgot your description of Mr Tilney: "a brown skin, with dark eyes, and rather dark hair." Well, my taste is different. I prefer light eyes; and as to complexion—do you know—I like a sallow better than any other. You must not betray me, if you should ever meet one of your acquaintance answering that description.'

'Betray you! What do you mean?'

'Nay, do not distress me. I believe I have said too much. Let us drop the subject.'

Catherine, in some amazement, complied; and after remaining a few moments silent, was on the point of reverting to what interested her at that time rather more than anything else in the world—Laurentina's skeleton—when her friend prevented her by saying, 'For Heaven's sake, let us move away from this end of the room. Do you know, there are two odious young men who have been staring at me this half-hour. They really put me quite out of countenance. Let us go and look at the arrivals. They will hardly follow us there.'

Away they walked to the book; and while Isabella examined the names, it was Catherine's employment to watch the proceedings of these alarming young men.

'They are not coming this way, are they? I hope they are not so impertinent as to follow us. Pray let me know if they are coming. I am determined I will not look up.'

In a few moments Catherine, with unaffected pleasure, assured her that she need not be longer uneasy, as the gentlemen had just left the Pump Room.

'And which way are they gone?' said Isabella, turning hastily round. 'One was a very good-looking young man.'

'They went towards the churchyard.'

'Well, I am amazingly glad I have got rid of them! And now, what say you to going to Edgar's Buildings with me, and looking at my new hat? You said you should like to see it.'

Catherine readily agreed. 'Only,' she added, 'perhaps we may over-take the two young men.'

'Oh! never mind that. If we make haste, we shall pass by them presently, and I am dying to show you my hat.'

'But if we only wait a few minutes, there will be no danger of our seeing them at all.'

'I shall not pay them any such compliment, I assure you. I have no notion of treating men with such respect. *That* is the way to spoil them.'

Catherine had nothing to oppose against such reasoning; and

therefore, to show the independence of Miss Thorpe, and her resolution of humbling the sex, they set off immediately as fast as they could walk, in pursuit of the two young men.

Exercises

1 The scene is Bath in the early nineteenth century. Collect information on the place and the period from sources such as Trevelyan's *Illustrated Social History*.
2 What was 'The Pump Room'?
3 Catherine and Isabella discuss a group of novels. What can you find out about these?
4 Discuss the sequence of events in this scene, and then list the various episodes.
5 Re-read the first paragraph. To what extent does the scene in fact reveal a 'warm attachment' or 'originality of thought' or 'literary taste'?
6 Improvise the following: Two friends meet in a coffee bar; one is five minutes late; they have a great deal to tell each other, especially about a series of programmes they have been watching on television.
   They also have some more basic reason for visiting the café—perhaps just to look at the girls, or to show off their fine suits of clothes. Vary the basic reason and then discuss how the change of reason affects the way they discuss the programmes. In each improvisation there should be genuine enthusiasm to discuss the programmes.
7 How does Isabella react to Catherine being slightly late? What is the possible reason for her reaction?
8 The two ladies appear to discuss a great variety of topics. Do these topics have anything in common?
9 Improvise the following: The scene is a holiday camp; it is a warm summer's morning; two young ladies sit in deck chairs overlooking the swimming pool; they met for the first time only the other day; they have a cool drink and chat in a somewhat idle and unenthusiastic fashion. . . .
10 On the other side of the swimming pool two young men, who also have only recently met, sit in deck chairs and chat in a somewhat idle and unenthusiastic fashion. . . .

11 What do the conversations in the two improvisations have in common? Do they have anything in common with the conversation between Isabella and Catherine?

12 Where would you set the scene if you wanted to get an exact modern parallel to early nineteenth-century Bath?

13 What novels would girls like Isabella and Catherine be reading today? What would be their tastes in cinema, television, theatre, music, fashion?

14 Tell someone, in detail, about a very fine friend of yours, preferably someone whom the listener does not know at all. Now ask the listener to tell someone else about your friend. Do you find that the listener has in fact got the picture right? Has he picked up more or less than you wanted him to? What picture does the reader get of Miss Andrews from Isabella's description? Is this the picture that Isabella might have meant us to receive? Is it the same picture as Catherine receives?

15 Think back to the last time when you actually told someone about one of your friends and praised the friend highly. What was the reason for telling about the friend? What is Isabella's reason for telling Catherine about Miss Andrews? Are there mixed reasons?

16 Why did Isabella insist that Captain Hunt should acknowledge that Miss Andrews is beautiful? Does she have an unconscious as well as a conscious reason?

17 Discuss the course of this particular session so far. Perhaps ask three people to leave the room and then ask each one in turn to return to give an account of the session from the moment when the extract from *Northanger Abbey* was read to the moment when this particular exercise was reached. What do you learn about the characters of the three people from the different accounts that they give? How far do you think it is true to say that we can discover a great deal about people from the things they find to talk about and comment on? How far, if at all, is this relevant to this text?

18 Make a list of virtues which Isabella attributes to herself. What evidence is there that she either possesses or does not possess these virtues?

19 Make a list of the faults which Isabella attributes to men. Why is she so keen to point out their faults?

20 After reading and studying the extract, do you feel keen to find the books which Isabella mentions and read them for yourself?

Does the answer to this question throw any light on the character of Isabella or the aims of the writer?

21 Does Isabella ever contradict herself?

22 How quickly can Isabella go from one subject to another?

23 What qualities would you look for in an actress auditioning for the part of Isabella? Is there any famous actress whom you would cast in the rôle?

4 When Isabella first tells Catherine about the two young men she refers to them as being 'odious'. Is this typical of her? Take the same basic situation—of two young girls apparently objecting to being looked at by two young men and pretending to walk away from them while actually hoping to attract and keep their attention—and improvise it in a very different time and place.

25 Improvise the scenes when the two ladies return home; how will Isabella narrate the morning's events to her mother? How will Catherine narrate the events to her hostess (Mrs Allen)?

26 The two ladies love reading romantic and rather melodramatic literature. How do you think such a scene as this—the morning in the Pump Room—would have been written by the authors of the ladies' favourite books? Perhaps read something by modern novelists such as Kathleen Winsor or Georgette Heyer, and then improvise the scene as it might have been written by these writers.

Improvisation and the technique of acting

All that has been suggested in this chapter about improvisation and the studying of a text applies of course to a group of actors working on a play for actual production. But improvisation can also be used to help develop the actor's technique:

(i) *Speech exercises* The company are given various exercises designed to improve their articulation. They improvise scenes in which they speak only in the sounds given in the exercise, obtaining emphasis only by the variations of pitch and rhythm. For example, have a cocktail party at which all the guests speak only in repeated consonants—der, der, der, ker, ker, ker, and so on. Very often, speech exercises are performed more effectively this way, where they become a joke, than they are when given purely as exercises.

(ii) *Vocal pitch and rhythm* If an actor is vocally monotonous, or is failing to pick up all the nuances of pitch and rhythm which every rôle demands, then he may become more sensitive to the whole idea of vocal variety if he is asked to do various exercises in improvisation. For instance, ask him to play an improvised sequence without altering at all the tone of his voice, and then without altering the pitch, and then the tempo. Give each actor in the sequence one specific instruction—not to change tempo, not to change pitch, and so on. Devise situations where sudden vocal changes are absolutely necessary. Then discuss the various changes called for in the actual text.

(iii) *Movement* Improvisation can often help to develop movement much more effectively than movement exercises themselves, if the situation in the improvisation is one that intrigues the actor. If for instance you are trying to develop a sense of style and elegance, devise numerous situations in which the actors are able to burlesque the kind of authority and panache you are looking for. Then devise situations in which the burlesque element is absent.

(iv) *Warm-ups* A lively session of improvisation is often a splendid way of starting a rehearsal. Use the whole group. Perhaps start off with nothing more elaborate than a birthday party at which someone makes too much noise and brings down the wrath of the neighbour. Such sessions can also be useful before an actual performance.

(v) *Listening* Many actors prove unable to listen to each other on stage. They may think they are listening to each other, but in fact they do not appear to be doing so from the audience. Ask an actor to watch other actors in any kind of improvisation and he will be given an example of real listening in a scene. Then put the actor into similar improvisations. Then discuss the various ways in which we listen in real life. Discuss the different degrees of listening. Discuss how far, if at all, we move about when we are listening.

(vi) *Period and style, situation and character* These are the aspects of the production which can most be helped by improvisation, and these have already been discussed in the earlier part of this chapter.

Postscript

Improvised drama is capable of endless variations. A few final suggestions:

(i) Improvisation based on paintings or photographs. The group is shown a picture and then improvises on some situation suggested by the picture.

(ii) Improvisation suggested by music. The group listens to a piece of music and then creates an improvisation suggested by the mood and feeling of the music. This does not necessarily mean that the music has to be played in the background.

(iii) Improvisation based on material in newspapers. The group reads through a newspaper and creates improvisations from ideas and material in the news.

(iv) Improvisation based on *Who, What, When, Where?* The basic instructions are given by the audience (the other groups):

WHO Each member of the group is given an identity, whether in the form of a trade or profession, or of a general description.

WHERE The scene is given a definite locality.

WHEN A time is given.

WHAT The opening line of dialogue is given.

(v) Improvisation based on a given title. The group is given a title such as *Gazornenplatt* or *Poor Old Joe* and then improvise freely around that title.

(vi) Improvisations based on themes, such as *The Future*—full-length revues and documentaries can be devised in this way.

(vii) *Group Story-telling* A group tell a story, partly through narrative, partly through improvised acting. Members of the group spontaneously take over the telling of the story from each other as they are going along, and alter the story as they see fit. In the same fashion they dramatise spontaneously with each other as they go along. All you need to begin with is someone to start off a story.